Autotelic Architect

Autotelic Architect explores how the new movement towards self-initiated projects, greater collaboration and design activism have changed how architects and designers are practising, as well as the kinds of projects they are working on. Similar to the autotelic self that transforms potential problems into enjoyable challenges, the 'Autotelic Architect' does not avoid societal changes, but instead learns to harness their creative potential. Using new research and case studies from past and present, the author analyses the educational and professional implications of operating as a 'non-conventional', progressive, participatory design practice. Drawing on a range of global case studies of pioneering architects in the field, she reflects upon current and future trends at the local, national and international levels, and additionally examines marketing, business and practical issues for architects. Illustrated with more than 30 black-and-white images, this is a compelling read for any practising architect.

Sumita Sinha is an alumni of five architecture schools from two continents, including Delhi, Cambridge, London South Bank, Manchester and Westminster. She has designed furniture and buildings, and has worked and taught in the fields of sustainable design, conservation and planning for over 20 years in nine countries. She has set up an architectural charity, Charushila. She has been associated with RIBA for over 20 years in various capacities, including setting up its equality forum and as a Council member. Currently she is also a non-executive director of Moorfields NHS Foundation Trust. This is her second book.

Autotelic Architect
Changing world,
changing practice

Sumita Sinha

LONDON AND NEW YORK

First published 2017
by Routledge
2 Park Square, Milton Park, Abingdon, Oxon OX14 4RN

and by Routledge
711 Third Avenue, New York, NY 10017

Routledge is an imprint of the Taylor & Francis Group, an informa business

© 2017 Sumita Sinha

The right of Sumita Sinha to be identified as author of this work has been asserted by her in accordance with sections 77 and 78 of the Copyright, Designs and Patents Act 1988.

All rights reserved. No part of this book may be reprinted or reproduced or utilised in any form or by any electronic, mechanical, or other means, now known or hereafter invented, including photocopying and recording, or in any information storage or retrieval system, without permission in writing from the publishers.

Trademark notice: Product or corporate names may be trademarks or registered trademarks, and are used only for identification and explanation without intent to infringe.

British Library Cataloguing-in-Publication Data
A catalogue record for this book is available from the British Library

Library of Congress Cataloging-in-Publication Data
Names: Sinha, Sumita, author.
Title: Autotelic architect : changing world, changing practice / Sumita Sinha.
Description: New York : Routledge, 2016. | Includes bibliographical references and index.
Identifiers: LCCN 2016001209| ISBN 9781138820425 (hardback : alk. paper) | ISBN 9781138820432 (pbk. : alk. paper) | ISBN 9781315743899 (ebook)
Subjects: LCSH: Architectural practice.
Classification: LCC NA1995 .S56 2016 | DDC 720.1--dc23
LC record available at http://lccn.loc.gov/2016001209

ISBN: 978-1-138-82042-5 (hbk)
ISBN: 978-1-138-82043-2 (pbk)
ISBN: 978-1-315-74389-9 (ebk)

Typeset in Sabon and Lucida Sans
by GreenGate Publishing Services, Tonbridge, Kent

Contents

List of illustrations		vi
Foreword by Peter Murray		viii
	Introduction	1
1	Changing world, changing practice	9
2	Practice of architecture	49
3	The autotelic education	87
4	The autotelic architect: practising architecture in a changing world	125
	Bibliography	173
	Index	177

Illustrations

Figures

1.1	Sir John Soane appears in the train toilet of Chiltern Railways	10
1.2	The promise of technology	11
1.3	The front of the RIBA building	20
1.4	The City of London is fast becoming overwhelmed by skyscrapers	22
1.5	An early twentieth-century pub demolished for new housing in West London	29
1.6	Construction work around the former BBC studios	30
1.7	Modern architecture travelled around the world regardless of context, climate and society in the 1950s	34
1.8	The roof of a house collapses in a busy shopping street, West London, after Storm Desmond in 2015	42
1.9	Spikes to deter the homeless in central London	44
2.1	New architecture dominates the area around the old Bank of England	51
2.2	The first iMac	61
2.3	Private house in Ealing, London, converted from an ordinary, two-storey house to look like the Palace of Versailles	63
2.4	Developer markets the contemporary 'architect designed home', London	64
2.5	As small business owners do not have the same resources to market their service or product as big businesses, they may have to be extra clever in winning over the competition	73
2.6	Protestors in front of the Chinese embassy	78

Illustrations   vii

3.1	Design courses are marketed to appeal to the heart	102
3.2	The 'recycled' office of charity Oasis, London	108
3.3	The Frank Lloyd Wright School of Architecture, Taliesin West	113
3.4	DIY architectural dialogue	114
3.5	Shrinarayan Hindu temple, Neasden, London	118
4.1	A sixth floating accommodation vessel arrived in Lerwick, Shetland, in 2014	127
4.2	Rising sea levels in places like Venice threaten to destroy more than a thousand years of architectural heritage	131
4.3	The Sea Organ and Greeting to the Sun by Nikola Bašić	133
4.4	'Care home' for the elderly, Orestad, Copenhagen	136
4.5	Chilean architect Smiljan Radić designed the fourteenth Serpentine Pavilion in 2014	137
4.6	Transferable technology in the form of quick sandbag construction as used in California has been transported to a school in West London	139
4.7	Four renovated Jubilee line train carriages have become offices in the non-profit venture, Village Underground, in East London	140
4.8	Ludwig Guttmann Healthcare Centre	142
4.9	City-centre parks provide an oasis for humans and animals	145
4.10	The Staircase by Supermachine, Thailand	149
4.11	The London Eye was designed by a team led by architects David Marks and Julia Barfield	151
4.12	UAL campus for Central Saint Martins	153
4.13	High Line Project by Diller Scofidio+Renfro, New York	154
4.14	A retrofit housing project using insulation made from discarded clothes	156
4.15	A retrofit of a home in a conservation area by Marks Barfield Architects	157
4.16	Another pop-up! TREExOFFICE in Hoxton Square, London	159
4.17	Wunderland Kalkar is an amusement park near Düsseldorf, Germany	166

Table

1.1	Architects' salaries and the cost of living index	35

Foreword

The opening line of *An Outline of European Architecture*, Nikolaus Pevsner's aphorism that 'A bicycle shed is a building, Lincoln Cathedral is a piece of architecture', has been read and digested by almost every first-year architecture student of the post-war period; but it set them off in a confusing direction. Totally different, of course, to artists who had long taken up Marcel Duchamp's wider definition of what is art. 'I don't believe in art. I believe in artists,' he said.

As a result of the sort of attitudes embodied in Pevsner's quotation, in the period of my working life, we have seen a diminution of the architect's role in the process of delivering buildings, while at the same time this narrowing of ambition has pushed others to investigate the less conventional methodologies that are documented in this book.

The narrowing of ambition and influence has been evident throughout my working life. In the 1970s, I was Technical Editor of *Architectural Design* magazine. Each year we put together the programme for the Architects Benevolent Society's Christmas Ball – the charity's major fundraising event. Everybody queued up to go in it, contractors, quantity surveyors and engineers of all kinds; all these people depended on architects for their livelihood. The tables at the Ball were paid for by other consultants wanting to host tables on which they could entertain architects. The Ball no longer takes place because other consultants stopped entertaining architects at their tables. They did not need to as the architects' influence on their commissions waned.

When I started as Editor of *Building Design* a few years later, it was stuffed full of advertisements because all product manufacturers wanted to attract the architect's attention. No one else really counted as far as specification was concerned. The contractor or QS might have had a say on suppliers of concrete or drainage goods, but little else. Today the amount of advertising in the architectural press is a fraction of what it was, reflecting the fact that now contractors and project managers are likely to have just as big a role in specification as the designer.

While I was researching my book *The Saga of the Sydney Opera House*, Jack Zunz, Chief Engineer at Arup working on the project, told me that one of the key reasons why engineers did not question Jorn Utzon's early concepts for the project was because 'then, the architect was the leader of the building team'. Back in the 1960s, what the architect said, went. The engineers just followed orders. The boot is on the other foot today.

In the 1980s when I edited the *RIBA Journal*, the President of the Institute was Chairman of the Group of eight construction industry organisations who met regularly with the Prime Minister to press their case on government construction policy. Today, RIBA does not have a single representative on the Construction Leadership Council that is implementing the industrial strategy for construction.

The architectural profession has not responded to changing circumstance to maintain control of an industry that they commanded at the start of my career. In architectural education, design has become central to what students are taught to do and taught to want to do – and the quality of design has certainly improved as a result. However, many of the other skills in putting up buildings have been ignored; subjects such as project management, supervision and a real understanding of the construction process. This has allowed other professionals to get into the powerful decision-making roles that were once held by architects. As the world has changed around them, the architect's role has contracted. Quantity surveyors have morphed into 'built asset consultants'. The bean counters are controlling large areas of work once the preserve of the architectural profession.

The development of Building Information Modelling (BIM) provided a golden chance for the profession to once again grab hold of the leadership of the profession, but it is too late. Other sectors of the industry took the initiative to invest and took a risk to control the process.

The IE University in Madrid, home to one of the world's leading business schools, offers a master's degree course on running an architectural business. Students from around the world – Australia, Mexico, Brazil, Russia, Canada – come to study specifically designed management strategies for practice. The only UK students who attend are those given scholarships, reflecting a perception that harks back to the mentality of Edwardian professionalism that business x Foreword

was beneath the architect. One of the most important architects of the post-war period – Neave Brown, designer of Alexandra Road in Camden – recently admitted in an interview in *AA Files* that in his practice he was 'flying blind'. A lack of business understanding meant he lost jobs and had no strategy to find jobs. The result? Brown has built only one important building in Britain and a couple in mainland Europe. What a waste of talent! Attitudes are changing, but the number of architects who still boast of 'flying blind' is alarming. What they do not understand is that an understanding of management and business provides greater freedom to determine the future of a practice and the types of work undertaken, not a capitulation to the profit motive.

As a student, I worked on Buckminster (Bucky) Fuller's World Design Decade project. Bucky wanted architecture students to help him plot the catastrophic wastage of the world's resources and assist in the development of a future for 'Spaceship Earth' and an ecosystem that predated much of the sustainability debate of recent years. He thought architects had the capacity to take on a wider role in helping to deliver a more sustainable environment and a fairer society.

Sumita's statistic that 97 per cent of new buildings in the world are designed without architects is very depressing. The profession has focused its work too narrowly and failed to meet the needs of large sections of modern society. At the same time, education and practice have failed to keep pace with modern management techniques and business practice, resulting in low levels of remuneration and an inability to adapt to the changing marketplace and new opportunities. However, despite all this, I remain convinced that the holistic thinking that emerges from project-based learning and what Donald Schon called 'reflective practice', their passion and commitment to improving lives, and their skills at making and making things happen, provide a unique blend of skills that can be harnessed to a wider range of tasks.

This overdue book takes a fresh look at the purpose of an architectural education – how architects can use their skills both to satisfy their own business needs and for the wider good. This involves an understanding of what architecture is and what architects do. Yes, we still need the formal statements that embody the characteristics that elevated Lincoln Cathedral in Pevsner's lexicon, but we also need good bike sheds. As the number of cyclists in cities increases exponentially, the accommodation of bicycle parking is a major issue and needs to be properly addressed.

I end this foreword with the story of an architect who has taken Pevsner's humble building type and had a real impact on street design in cities around the world. Anthony Lau won a competition at the 2006 London Festival of Architecture for the design of the Cyclehoop secure bicycle parking system. From this beginning, Lau has built up a major business delivering a wide range of equipment and street furniture that is elegant and functional and meets a real need – including an on-street bike shed!

Peter Murray

Introduction

I thought I should start with defining 'autotelic' first.[1] 'Autotelic' derives from the Greek words *auto*, meaning 'self', and *telos*, meaning 'goal'. Autotelic activity is about having a purpose in and not apart from itself. Applied to personality types, autotelic denotes an individual who generally does things for their own sake, rather than in order to achieve an external goal.[2] It is not a new word though – the *Oxford English Dictionary* cites its earliest use as 1901[3] and also cites a 1932 use by T.S. Eliot.[4] So the word 'autotelic' is over a century old. The autotelic personality is a yin–yang person – a combination of receptive qualities such as openness and flexibility, as well as active qualities such as engagement and persistence.

While the definition of autotelic can give an impression of a lone worker, stranded in an attic, working away all hours, in reality the autotelic worker will be someone who is not immune to external forces but who uses those as creative challenges much like the martial art of ju-jutsu where someone uses the attacker's energy against them. In fact, the 'ju' here stands for all sorts of unaggressive expressions, such as gentle, soft, supple, flexible, pliable or yielding. So being autotelic is not about being combative but about being collaborative, motivated not by anger but by creativity, and finding fulfilment by self-directed goals, not external influences. Autotelic working is smart working. Autotelic work is proactive, not reactive.

Self-concordant goals according to research from Kennon Sheldon and Andrew Elliot[5] are integrated with the self because they come from 'self-choice'. Externally directed goals make us stressed and depressed, while self-directed ones are those that give us joy and ease. Self-chosen goals also stem from the need to express one's creativity and spirit rather than simply do the work. Research in this area indicates that there is a qualitative difference between the meaning we derive from extrinsic goods, such as social status and salary, and the meaning we derive from intrinsic goods, such as personal growth and

2 Introduction

a sense of connection to others. Our choices can be a mixture of both self-directed and externally directed goals as long as the self-directed goal directs the external manifestation of it. The autotelic architect's problem perhaps is not that of generating creativity but of continuously balancing the external aims of financial stability, success and recognition with the internal desires of creativity, perseverance and motivation.

Most work can be divided crudely into three categories: creative, contributive and commercial. Creative work is work that is done for pleasure – it is what we love doing. Creative work can be either a hobby or paid work. Contributive work is a service carried out in society, such as the work of teachers, doctors, nurses, bus drivers, etc. This kind of work has medium-to-high pay. Commercial work is selling or making products on a large scale (industrial) or dealing with money (banking). Each type includes some aspect of the other – for instance, teaching is a contributive work that involves some creativity. A photographer can be contributive as well as commercial. Commercial work may involve a contributive element through the aspect of corporate social responsibility. Tsunesaburo Makiguchi, the Japanese philosopher, called a creative life a 'contributive life'. His premise was that in order to realise individual well-being, one needs to have a cooperative and contributive existence within society. According to Alain de Botton, '[a job feels meaningful] whenever it allows us to generate delight or reduce suffering in others'.[6] But, he says that 'we should be wary of restricting the idea of meaningful work too tightly, of focusing only on doctors, nuns of Kolkata or the Old Masters'.[7] Autotelic work ideally can be creative, contributive and commercially viable. Architects do creative work, but can they be contributive and commercial as well?

I noticed that, during 2013–2015, several new publications and reviews about new ways of 'doing' or valuing the profession arrived in quick succession. There was a 2015 parliamentary inquiry into the value of design; the 2015 Royal Institute of British Architects (RIBA) review of architectural education; the 2014 Farrell report on architecture; books such as *Disruptive Design Practice Handbook*[8] and *21 Things You Won't Learn in Architecture School*;[9] and, to top it, an animated short series about the life of a frustrated architect named Archibald started on YouTube[10] in 2014. There had been other rumblings before, such as *Other Ways of Doing Architecture*,[11] and many booklets about the value of architecture or design published by the Commission for Architecture and the Built Environment (CABE). But this appeared to be an avalanche – something was definitely shifting. This architectural climate change interested me immensely. First, I wanted to know if it would or had already affected me and, second, I wanted to investigate its seriousness and consequences. What was happening? Did we see it coming? Or like rabbits caught in the glare of the headlights, were we frozen at the shock of it all?

So I started to look at history to find out whether this sort of thing had happened before and what our response had been to it. What I discovered was that not only had such acute challenges gripped our profession from time to time but that architects had managed not just to survive but also prosper and give back to society. Best of all, I discovered that architects who enjoy such challenges are still to be found. These were autotelic architects. Similar to the autotelic self that translates potential threats into enjoyable challenges, the autotelic architect enjoys obstacles and turns threats into opportunities. The challenges of the rapidly changing context of the twenty-first century are for professionals who accept pluralism, ambiguity and paradox as part of life and use them as 'creative abrasion'[12] to push ahead.

I found that these survivors were not just passionate about architecture but also passionate about running a business. Simply loving something is not going to run a business, no matter what the new-age business books say. For architecture is a time-intensive and poor-paying profession. I was aged 13 and living in India when I declared that I wanted to be an architect and my father said: 'But you'll never earn any money – it's far better to be a doctor.' So I passed both my medical and architecture entrance exams to make a point but chose the latter (to make another point). As a profession, we are lucky that we can study and work almost anywhere in the world for different organisations and related sectors. Skills and learning can be transferable too thanks to some uniformity in the global validation of the course (but not employment as I was to find out). After I completed Parts 1 and 2 in architecture in Delhi and won an international design competition, I worked in Delhi for a housing agency and, later, for a small rural practice in France. So far I have worked and taught in nine different countries and have been the alumni of five different schools of architecture on two different continents. I have been able to work in different genres from 'low-energy architecture', conservation, interior design, housing and offices to urban regeneration in different-sized practices.

4 Introduction

As far as the 'commercial aspect' of being an architect, my total lack of business skills despite having Part 3 was made apparent when I decided to start on my own. So I completed a business course and started with the great disadvantage of being new to the UK with no contacts in a profession that is based heavily on networking. Armed with the confidence and energy of youth, I was practising and teaching when the first recession hit the UK. I also completed a diploma in teaching. Having children made me realise that being a carer and having a career did not always work out. Wishing to make a contribution, I became Chair of the group Women in Architecture and then set up Architects for Change, RIBA's equality forum in 2000.

Now I have become what Charles Handy has called a 'portfolio worker' – besides my small design practice, I also started an architectural charity, Charushila, which has worked internationally. I teach from time to time and sit on the board of an NHS Foundation Trust. (Why NHS? Because they needed an architect and so, in a roundabout way, I also fulfilled my father's dream of being in the medical profession.) I also do other fun things on the side such as art and photography exhibitions, writing and acting. Life has taught me not to put all my eggs in one basket. I saw that many others were working in the same way, with at least a couple of eggs in many baskets. And also this was nothing new – that in the past, architects have always had many careers. I realised how the architect's education is a very versatile one – it enables a person to have many eggs to put in the basket in the first place. It enables a person to have a choice, unlike other professions.

However, the way that clients choose *us* now has changed. Where the public choose to live and what they choose to put in their homes have changed. In 1959, President Richard Nixon of the USA had an insightful exchange with his counterpart in the USSR, Nikita Khrushchev, when they went around the American trade exhibition in Moscow before the official opening. They saw the USSR's display of technological power first, a replica of the world's first satellite, Sputnik I. Next they went to the display from the USA, which turned out to be a mock-up of a kitchen with the latest gadgets – washing machines, toasters and juicers. In an exchange captured by the CIA, Khrushchev dismissed it: 'You Americans expect that the Soviet people will be amazed. It is not so. We have all these things in our new flats.' Nixon responded: 'We do not claim to astonish the Soviet people. We hope to show our right to choose. We do not wish to have decisions made at the top by government officials who say that all homes should be built in the same way.'

Introduction   5

It is ironic that the foremost capitalist country in the world used a kitchen to demonstrate choice in a free market economy against Soviet-built technology and mass housing while, nearly 60 years later, our mass housing only demonstrates a lack of choice and imagination. Today, our 'social fitness markers' do not include well-designed homes but include other tangible acquisitions, such as smart phones, flat screen TVs and flat pack disposable furniture. The rise of the 'experience economy' and sharing of those mean that concrete things such as homes and interiors do not matter to Joe Public. The architectural profession is seen as a luxury, not a necessity like that of a doctor (who cares if architects were to go on strike?!).

Public bodies, which are under pressure to 'save' money, view architects as unnecessary today, unlike in the Golden Era of social housing leading up to the 1970s. But architects remain curiously content that architecture is important to society. Yet the fact that we are paid less than office workers, and sometimes not even paid, might indicate that our work is not valued, and that we should get our heads out of the concrete. Equally, my experience of being at RIBA for more than 20 years, which includes being on the Council and sitting on many committees – international, practice and profession, ethics, etc. – has reinforced my view that RIBA has to support architects more strongly than before. Further architectural education, which also saw its own reviews, is facing unprecedented challenges, bringing further problems to students who are brave enough to study it. Again, I believe that RIBA has to support them too.

We have to admit that we are pretty weak as agents of change. Humans spend 90 per cent of their time inside buildings and, yet, only 2–3 per cent of the world's buildings are designed by architects. We do not have a union to campaign for improving work conditions or pay and, because architects do not earn much money, we end up working all hours, without much regard for our health and sanity. I was anxious to find out who speaks for architects. Architects are now competing to design on the tiniest spaces, from shop windows to beach huts – and it is difficult to make a living, let alone run an office. No wonder we are either concocting new projects or taking part in expensive competitions or speculative work. A fellow architect said, not without irony: 'It is a great discipline and a very difficult profession (and a nearly impossible business!).'

Someone asked me: 'Are you writing about architecture or about architects?' Both, I answered, because in our present circumstances

6 Introduction

one does not exist without the other (although historically buildings have always existed without architects). We realise that the system is wrong but we are spending time and money in tweaking things here and there in the hope that things will improve – some lobbying, some reviews and some television programmes. And we are looking in the wrong places in order to improve. Like the drunk looking for keys not where he lost them but under the street lamp 'because the light is better there',[13] we might be looking at the wrong places to improve our business. We need to look elsewhere for answers, to re-examine the profession from outside in – from the standpoint of our clients – to run our business efficiently and value our own time and life (even if we are healthy).

I wrote this book, because I am on the journey to find out what the profession can be. *But I didn't want this book to be about 'how to do successful architecture' or 'step-by-step' problem solving or even how to have many eggs in one basket.* I have tried not to bring in new-age advice from business books – first because architects do not like to be advised and, second, these ideas usually do not have any relevance to our ways of working. As Nichiren, the thirteenth-century Japanese monk, advised: 'It is like the case of a poor man who spends night and day counting his neighbor's wealth but gains not even half a coin.'[14] I have to add that this book unashamedly borrows from the experiences of, and favours, the small practice. Why? Because they are the largest types of practice in the world, and so it would be good to highlight the valuable work and business practices of small organisations.

This book is for reflection on the state of the profession and, hopefully, a 'good news' book too. It looks in honest and open ways at some difficult issues in our profession and then takes inspiration from the many ways that architects around the globe have transformed their practices and the world around them. I have learnt many things from writing this book, including how similar writing a book is to designing a building. And now having lived with writing this for some time, in the words of a fellow architect, Thomas Hardy, I shall

> pick up the drawing that slipped from my hand,
> And feel for the pencil I dropped in the cranny,
> In a moment of forgetfulness.[15]

Introduction 7

Acknowledgements

Writing can be a lonely task but, in this virtual world, I have to thank the hundreds of people from all professions who responded to my posts on social media and sent me valuable comments, illustrations and contacts. I am very grateful for their frank and sincere contributions.

I would like to acknowledge the contributions from my colleagues at work and at those at RIBA and the ARB, past students and creative friends who contributed to the 'creative soirées' I organised. In particular, I'd like to thank Professor Mike McEvoy, Roger Kelly, Amanda Reekie, Richard Brindley and Adrian Dobson who generously gave me their time and thoughts but did not stop me from expressing my views, different those might be to theirs. I would like to thank some of my teachers from India and the UK – Professors M.R. Agnihotri, Satish Grover and Ross Jamieson and Dr Martin Cowley – all sadly passed away now – and Dr Nick Baker. All who have encouraged me as a student and also in practice through the years. My thanks to Peter Murray who took time to write the foreword, which not only collates all my thoughts but also adds a perspicacious layer to it. And thank you to my publishers, Routledge.

I thank my family for patiently putting up with me while I wrote another book.

Finally I thank those autotelic architects from past and present, whose compelling stories run through this book and inspired me.

Notes

1 An architect wrote as a response to my LinkedIn article: 'I must admit that if you hadn't kindly included the definition of "autotelic", I would have had to reach for the [online] dictionary, but I would have been intrigued enough to do so, and discovered a rich new wor[l]d in the process. Yes, I do think that we are being "dumbed down" by a commodity culture that seeks to simplify and "flatten" words and meanings so that "people" don't have to make the effort to think and question and are left with more time to passively consume.'
2 Csikszentmihalyi (1997, p. 117). 'The mark of the autotelic personality is the ability to manage a rewarding balance between the "play" of challenge finding and the "work" of skill building' (Csikszentmihalyi *et al.*, 1993, p. 80).
3 J.M. Baldwin (1901).
4 T.S. Elliot, *Essays* I. ii. 24, http://link.springer.com/article/10.1007%2 FBF02089750 (accessed February 2015).

8   Introduction

5 http://web.missouri.edu/~sheldonk/pdfarticles/JCCP04.pdf   (accessed August 2015). A total of 551 college undergraduates participated in the study – 194 South Korean students from Hanyang University in Seoul, South Korea; 153 US students from the University of Missouri in Columbia, Missouri; 163 Taiwanese students from the National Sun Yat-Sen University in Kaohsiung, Taiwan; and 41 Chinese students from the Guangdon Commercial College in Guangzhou, South China.
6 A. de Botton (2010, p. 78).
7 Ibid., p. 80.
8 Moser (2014).
9 Dobson (2014).
10 www.youtube.com/user/archmaaikcom. arch. is a weekly online cartoon series by Mike Hermans, an Antwerp-based architect–cartoonist, that follows Archibald through the struggles architects know. Archibald is a self-professed 'visionary and romantic dreamer', while his business partner Gerald is the anti-creative in a constant struggle to ground Archibald's ideas in reality.
11 Aswan *et al.* (2011).
12 Creative abrasion is a phrase coined by Jerry Hirshberg, founder and president of Nissan Design International, and describes a culture where differing or contrasting inputs are not rejected but used to further creativity.
13 Abraham Maslow (1954, p. 16) referenced this anecdote in his text *Motivation and Personality* – the origins of this story that started in the twentieth century are unknown.
14 Nichiren Daishonin, *Major Writings*, Volume 1, p. 4, 1255 CE.
15 Wright (1978, p. 126).

1 Changing world, changing practice

There really is no such thing as an architect. There is only architecture.

Paraphrasing E.H. Gombrich's original words[1] about art to architecture became for me a way to explore the origins of architecture, particularly that of the architect. In Gombrich's book though, art is synonymous with architecture. He categorises architecture as a form of art: 'I shall discuss the history of art, that is the history of building, of picture making and of statue making.'[2] He describes architecture essentially as utilitarian art, some of which may be more exciting and beautiful than others.[3] Colin Wilson describes architecture as a form of 'representational art',[4] while Samuel Mockbee described it as 'social art'.[5] Today, Guernsey[6] does not recognize the architect as a profession but as a 'master craftsman'. The Turner prize, which is given to the best visual artist under the age of 50, was won in 2015 by the architecture and design collective, Assemble. On the other hand, there are also non-architects who aspire to design buildings and structures.[7] It perhaps reinforced the view that architecture is maybe more akin to art, but is it? There is of course art in how buildings are designed and put together. With knowledge of proportions and materials, there is a bit of an artist in every architect. Kenneth Clark (1999), in his book *Civilisation*, says that architects through history who were artists made better architects. But that is not the entire story – the reality is a bit more complicated. Architecture is more than the sum of these confines – utilitarian, social, technical or representational. To understand architecture and the profession, we will have to understand the people who practise it – the architects.

Who is an architect? Why do we need architects? The answers are perhaps more complex than the answers to: 'Who is a doctor?' 'Why do we need doctors?' As a profession we are new, and so is our course of studies. But buildings and structures have existed without architects – even animals and insects can build homes, colonies, defences and dams. Slums and shanty towns exist all over the globe, without

Figure 1.1 Sir John Soane appears in the train toilet of Chiltern Railways. In 2013, train toilets were fitted with floor-to-ceiling vinyl images to coincide with the attractions to be found on the London–Birmingham route. However, not many people using the toilet recognised Sir John

Source: Clare Crosland.

Figure 1.2 The promise of technology was captured in this mural made by the artist Gordon Cullen in the listed Greenside school which was designed by Erno Goldfinger and built in 1952. Images include the first commercial jet, the de Havilland Comet, first flown in 1951, and the Britannia 70000, the first standard steam locomotive commissioned by the Railways Board and rolled out in 1951

Source: author.

12 Changing world, changing practice

the need for architects; and planners and vernacular expressions of the built form have always been around. Around 97 per cent[8] of the world's architecture is built by non-architects, and two-thirds of the UK's planning permissions are applied for by non-architects.

Creativity for architects is not just an intrinsic quality – we are dependent upon external ideas and references as well as innovations from engineers, scientists and materialogists that we string together for design and construction. Despite the optimism of the *Yellow Book*[9] produced by students of the Architectural Association in 1937 that 'social, technical and cultural processes offer limitless possibilities for architectural invention', neither architects nor their clients are able to make use of this limitless creative freedom – most work is really a reference to the past. We don't make jumps, we take baby steps (like our clients). Unlike artists, architects are bound by context and the ephemerality of politics and economy, not least the client's desires. While the more flamboyant expressions of modern architecture certainly get press coverage, their failure to be enduring icons of public admiration and even technical robustness do not validate them as utilitarian art. Talking about Assemble's Turner prize win, a critic responded:[10]

> Why bring it in as art? If you're just looking for stuff that isn't pretentious and is useful, why don't you nominate B&Q or Oxfam? It's great if art can be useful. But just because it's useful doesn't make it art.

As artists, our work speaks to a very limited audience, and perhaps that is why mass housing, for instance, continues to be built in iterations of the historic styles. That is not innovative. Our artistic and creative expressions may be limited but our social presence is vast. It is as people of the community that we must first speak.

Many books, reviews and conferences testify to the enduring fascination with whether architecture is art or science and its role in 'place-making'. However, my question is more about whether architecture is a profession. The dilemma might be that while we think of ourselves as professionals, others see us as artists only. If it is art, then we must accept the consequences of being artists and the unspoken rules that go with that choice. But my analysis of both architectural practice and education shows that it is being practised and taught as a 'hobby', not as a profession. When an architect says that he spent one year discussing the design of a staircase within a larger project, it must beg the question as to how he supported himself, his family and his practice at that time. At least three architects (all female) said

Changing world, changing practice 13

that they did not pay themselves, only their staff, until they started making a profit – all were supported by a partner who worked in another profession until then. These impressions do not support a view that architecture is perceived as a business by those practising it. They confirm the view that architecture is an elitist profession – that only those who have other sources of income can afford to tinker with architectural work until it becomes profit-making. When I interviewed architects for this book, I got the impression that it was vulgar to talk about profits and losses. At RIBA's annual conference for small businesses, Guerilla Tactics, avoids we find many 'soft' topics such as leadership, branding, pitch, graphic design, etc.

It would appear from the study of the past that the image of the architect as a 'bohemian businessman' is a recent construct. It is certainly a romantic and appealing vision of a dilettante but restrictive and ultimately unfulfilling. Or perhaps, like the ostrich's head in the sand, we have a cognitive aversion to goals or even survival. Most creative businesses are risky work. For architects, the cost of indemnity insurance is proportionally more than that of doctors working for the NHS, for instance, and the threat of litigation is high while Construction (Design and Management) duties keep piling up. There are some professions who have protected or growing markets such as doctors and lawyers. But a 'creative profession' – and I can only think of one: architecture – is work done at risk. When one developer says that 'only architects give me art, creativity and excitement',[11] other developers have been accused of ruthless cost-cutting where design priorities have been put at the bottom by developers and design fees have been cut. In no other professions is there such a delicate balance between artistic freedom and scientific rigour held together with the stress of liability. In ancient Rome, the story goes that the designer or engineer had to stand under the structure as the scaffolding was taken off. It was literally an extreme post-occupancy design review. We are not subjected to such tests any more but the profession of architecture seems to be under threat both internally and externally. What is the architect's role in times of extreme change? Perhaps history can inform us.

In 1931, Chicago was in the midst of social and architectural upheavals. Criminal gangs and mafia, notably led by Al Capone, ruled the streets filled with 'speakeasies' (establishments selling alcohol illegally during the Prohibition era), racial tensions and shootings. At the height of the Great Depression, unemployment reached 50 per cent. But in the middle of all this, the city was building its skyscrapers – in total 25 were built by 1933 – and somehow the profession of architecture was flourishing. Four days before Christmas in 1931, a young

14 Changing world, changing practice

man named Richard Crews sent letters to the offices of several prominent Chicago architects inquiring about the demands of daily life in the profession. Four of the architects wrote back: Howard White, a founding member of Graham, Anderson, Probst & White (successors to D.H. Burnham & Co. and the largest architectural firm under one roof during the first half of the twentieth century); Chas Morgan, an associate of the more famous Frank Lloyd Wright; Ernest Braucher, who designed arts and crafts-style residences; and Clarence Doll. Chas Morgan responded: 'A real architect like a good man in any business does not waste any time whatsoever doing things of which he might be ashamed, he must above all be a sincere *artist*.'[12]

But the least known Doll came up with a very pragmatic response: 'An architect's work is quite varied from just drawing. He is much more of a business man than you may imagine, and for this reason a commercial course in his education is of great importance.'[13] Written almost 85 years ago during a time of great upheaval, these issues are now being debated by both practitioners and students. But Doll was not the first one to see architecture as a business – the ever pragmatic and successful Sir John Soane had categorised the responsibilities of an architect in 1788:

> The *business* of the architect is to make the designs and estimates, to direct the works and to measure and value the different parts; he is the intermediate agent between the employer, whose honour and interest he is to study, and the mechanic, whose rights he is to defend. His situation implies great trust; he is responsible for the mistakes, negligences, and ignorances of those he employs; and above all, he is to take care that the workmen's bills do not exceed his own estimates. If these are the duties of an architect, with what propriety can his situation and that of the builder, or the contractor be united?[14]

Sir John Soane is an example worth remembering. Despite being so business like about the work of an architect, he progressed in an autodidactic manner from being a lowly brick layer to a member of the Royal Academy, with his designs studied at schools of architecture even now. Perhaps he was the first autotelic architect.

The structure of the architectural profession

In 2014, a poll of architectural practices revealed that AECOM in the USA[15] became the first practice to employ more than 2,100 people

Changing world, changing practice **15**

and hold the position of the world's biggest practice – one-quarter more than the second-placed firm, Japanese practice Nikken Sekkei. Gensler, which was the year before's number one practice employing 1,614 architects, is presently in third place. The highest-placed British firm is Foster + Partners with 634 architects in 16th place, with the next highest UK practice being BDP in joint 32nd place with 358 architects. Indian, Korean, Singaporean and Chinese architectural practices also find places amongst the top 100. However, due to the vagaries of international exchange rates, the combined income of these Asian countries is much lower than their counterparts from Western nations[16] – £440,000 or less compared to £1.2 million. Although five of the world's largest firms are based in North America, with three in Asia and only one in the UK (Aedas, which ranked 5th, is dually based in both China and the UK), the UK has about half the number of employed architects as the USA. UK firms also earned almost as much in fee income – this discrepancy arising from global monetary value.[17] But these numbers are still comparatively very small compared with many other industries such as banking, advertising, etc.

Unlike the 1950s–1970s when most architects worked in the public sector, now most work is carried out in private offices in the UK and elsewhere. Most of these fall under the EU's 'small- and medium-sized enterprise'[18] (SME) category, even the largest ones. There are presently about 35,000 practising architects in the UK. The practices are categorised by RIBA's benchmarking survey as:

- micro: under 5;
- small: between 5 and 10;
- small to medium: 10–20;
- medium to large: 20–50;
- large: above 50.

The average architect's office is between 1 and 10 people and those constitute more than 60 per cent of British architects. Profit margins are small. In construction, despite project costs that run into millions generally, profit margins are as low as 2–3 per cent. Out of this small profit comes the architect's slice. While smaller practices can have 22 per cent profit, in larger practices this falls to 10 per cent due to their overheads. It is not surprising to read headlines about architectural practices that state turnover increases but profit declines, which in any other business would be ringing alarm bells but not ours (even

16 Changing world, changing practice

Sir Richard Roger's practice issued revenue warnings in 2016). Due to low profits, risk aversion is high, along with a general lack of interest and money towards research and innovation (and for PR).

Architects are also turning to other 'softer' sources of work, such as interior and furniture design. Unlike 'architect', 'interior designer' is not a protected term in the UK and therefore anyone is able to set up a practice and call themselves an interior designer regardless of qualifications or experience. Therefore, the British Institute of Interior Design (BIID), set up only in 1965, advises that clients should go through them to avoid charlatans. Many architects have also listed themselves in the BIID directory, as have non-EU architects who do not want to go through the process of registration due to the time and expense. Whether such shift in work is a threat in the UK to the 'traditional' architect's role remains to be assessed over time.

Today in the £1,664 billion construction market of the EU, architects take only a £14 billion slice, spread amongst 56,500 architects. Some 43 per cent of that market is new build and the rest is refurbishment, including retrofit. But the role of architects has become specialised and fragmented, within teams or as consultants, rather than leaders in a project. Now we have not just other cognate professionals' involvement in a project but also 'concept architects' and 'delivery architects'. The internal fragmentation of the profession also affects clients – for both large and small projects. The clients for small projects, particularly the domestic ones, seek out builders to fulfil the architect's vision, thus cutting their fees further. In the RIBA report 'Client and architect: Developing the essential relationship' published in September 2015, big clients said that they would like to see 'one-stop shops' with clients. However, the perceived financial advantages from not having an architect deliver the project may influence the market forces for a long time. Architectural design is now seen as a luxury by those who can afford it.[19] But this was not always the case.

Until the late 1970s, architects were big players, particularly those working in the public realm, constructing homes, schools, hospitals and infrastructure. In the 1950s, the London County Council architects boasted more than 1,500 architects. Re-building ruined cities after the devastation of two world wars, architects and town planners became important (if not totally loved) people in society through the 30 'golden decades of the welfare society' lasting until 1975. Architects were part of the social system, they weren't seen as removed from it as they are now. Social housing was also constructed in other war-damaged European countries such as Austria, the Netherlands, Sweden and Italy. The Byker Wall in Newcastle, for example, is a housing project designed by Ralph Erskine and built in the 1970s, now placed on UNESCO's list of outstanding twentieth-century buildings. It is an example of how a community worked with the architect and made it a successful and well-loved public housing project.

Some of these architects would also go out to build cities in the newly liberated colonies of Britain's golden era of social housing. Architectural movements such as modernism, post-modernism and other branches such as hi-tech, green and community architecture made architecture a talked-about subject. People lived in a new and equal social order, unlike in the older world where the classical and the vernacular divided the privileged and the poor. Architectural giants of the twentieth century such as Walter Gropius, Le Corbusier and Frank Lloyd Wright established ideas about the built environment that changed our world forever. Consequently, these ideas have had huge global effects and unintended consequences that are now being questioned.

But now it seems architects have become the scapegoats for any problems, according to those reviewing architecture. 'Britain risks repeating the mistakes of the post-war era if it doesn't take seriously the influence the built environment has on human behaviour,' said the chair of the All-Party Parliamentary Design and Innovation Group.[20] Modernist architecture also stands accused of elitism:

> It is ironic, yet somehow predictable, that modernism – fruit of the economic ruin by two world wars, enemy of aristocratic privilege, champion of efficiency over sentiment – should finally, with the neo-modernism of today, become the prestige style of the rich.[21]

A prominent architect has warned that Britain's global architectural dominance is at risk because students are studying the 'wrong subjects'.[22] Even architects are not beyond criticising each other – a well-known 'starchitect' reportedly[23] said: 'In the world we live in, 98 per cent of everything that's built and designed today is pure shit. There's no sense of design, no respect for humanity or for anything. They're bad buildings and that's it.' (Though he later attributed his remarks to jet lag.)

18 Changing world, changing practice

In 1962, RIBA published a report called 'The Architect and his [sic] Office'[24] which surveyed British architectural practices. This review arose from the criticism that not only were architects unable to manage their own affairs due to 'lack of proper management training' but also that of the client. This report, which looked into the professional management and practice of architects, found that the architects relied on 'intuition' rather than 'conscious management techniques'. It also caused RIBA to look into the delivery of architectural education.[25] One would like to think that more than half a century later, we have advanced a bit further but we seem to be still stuck – the RIBA 2013 benchmark survey showed that 62 per cent of practices do not have a business plan and, out of those, only 13 per cent plan beyond one year. It is not surprising to see so many complaints held against architects just on the simple things such as having a proper contract and writing notes. More than 50 years later, data has suggested that there appeared to be no correlation between success at winning work and profitability, suggesting practices are still chasing and winning projects at fees that were too low or that they were doing large amounts of unpaid speculative work.

Both speculative work and entering competitions as a means of establishing a name and winning work are tortuous routes to fame and fortune. In 2013, as much as 60 per cent of practices undertook speculative work which was unpaid. Clients often see this as a way to get 'free and innovative ideas'.[26] Many developers and architects can also spend much of their time and money working on speculative projects – millions of pounds may be spent on such projects (a developer I spoke to admitted spending £2 million on a speculative project in Central London). Another architect is happy to admit that he spends a lot of time not doing projects, i.e. working on speculative projects with a small team of 20 with offices based in the UK and China.[27] An architect I interviewed said that his office (one of the biggest in the UK) had spent £86,000 on a competition entry, which in the end did not win. Even a medium-sized architectural practice cannot afford to waste this kind of money. All competition work involves working on concepts and sometimes fairly detailed proposals that require a significant amount of time and money. A reader commented: 'No other profession is encouraged by its representative body to undertake at-risk work.' Despite this, architects enter competitions without commitment to transparency from the organisers and with onerous requirements from the competitor. In the end, poorly managed competitions only let down the clients who may end up with unbuildable projects.[28]

Australian architect Paul Wilson told me that in his opinion, 'competitions kill architecture'[29] and he has stopped participating in them. RIBA has said that it wants to see more better-run design competitions[30] after a review of the process. It set up a task group to look at how more architects can increase their chances of winning them as well as reducing the burden and cost of entering competitions. Despite the headlines, in 2013–2014, less than 1 per cent of new work was won through competitions.

The protection of the architect

We take the presence of architecture for granted as we look around us. Travelling to other countries invariably means looking at architecture. The word architect is derived from the 1550s, from Middle French *architecte*, from Latin *architectus* and from Greek *arkhitekton*, which means 'master builder, director of works', from *arkhi-* 'chief' + *tekton* 'builder, carpenter'. So the architect was always the 'action man'. So the original meaning of the word 'architect' has perhaps very different connotations to what we know of the work of an architect today. However, there has always been 'architecture without architects', a vernacular tradition where mostly the poor have lived. Kings to despots, and corporations, have used architecture to proclaim their power – through the use of superior materials or bigger structures. There are, of course, examples of many royals (and now celebrities) who took a keen interest (and continue to do so) in architecture and commissioned great projects, and became de facto architects by doing that, such as Akbar the Great, who is credited with the design of palaces and forts in India. A building's important relationship to civilisation and power can be summed up in the words of an ancient Egyptian 'architect': 'Build it correctly, all is well. Build it badly, all Egypt will fail.'[31] The profession, which is entirely a Western rationalisation, may have had its roots in the Renaissance when the idea of the 'architect-artist' that originated with many artists – usually Italian (Michelangelo, Leonardo, Bernini, Brunelleschi, etc.) – who moved between art and building. In time, the art side became more dominant than the building side – a shift that was to have great repercussions later in the profession as well as education. Builders and craftsmen were organised in guilds as early as medieval times – these would become later professional bodies or associations.

As far as the profession of architecture is concerned, it was only in the nineteenth century that architecture became delineated from other crafts such as carpentry, stone masonry, etc. and practised as a design

Figure 1.3 The front of the RIBA building. Its architect, George Grey Wornum, worked with a range of artists and craftsmen to create the decoration in the interiors and on the façade. The building was completed on time and on budget. The top carving by Edward Bainbridge is called 'Architectural Inspiration'

Source: author.

profession in both the UK and USA. The skilful use of 'modern' materials such as glass, concrete and steel in the nineteenth-century design by architects led to their recognition as those with technical skills. As cities expanded in the Industrial Revolution, architects and engineers worked together to build them. In the United States, Charles Bulfinch, the architect of the National Capitol Building in Washington, is the first person believed to have worked as a full-time professional architect and urban planner. Henry Hobson Richardson may have been one of the first to have an established office, and McKim, Mead & White may have been among the first to resemble a large architectural firm. The oldest active architecture firms in the United States are SmithGroup of Detroit and Luckett & Farley of Louisville, KY, both founded in 1853. In cities such as Chicago where the modern skyscraper originated, a number of architectural practices started, such as Skidmore, Owings & Merrill (SOM), which is still going as one of the largest firms in the world. In the United Kingdom, Brierley Groom is said to be the oldest continuing practice, founded in 1750 in York.

However, the profession was still unregulated and, in the nineteenth century, anyone could call themselves architects – and accidents on site and failed buildings were common. So in 1791, in order to distinguish between the charlatan and the professional, a private 'architect's club', which included John Soane, was formed. In 1834, this club eventually became the Institute of British Architects in London. It received the royal charter in 1837 and became known as the Royal Institute of British Architects. Its charter stated simply that RIBA's function was for 'the general advancement of Civil Architecture, and for promoting and facilitating the acquirement of the knowledge of the various arts and sciences connected therewith'.[32] So here lay the origins of a body for the advancement of architecture, but not the architect. This, as we shall see later, has turned out to be a bitter result. RIBA's building was only constructed in 1934 – 100 years after being set up. RIBA has had, and continues to have, influence not only in the UK but also its former colonies (covering two-thirds of the globe) and others. The word 'chartered' carries with it connotations of professional superiority. RIBA also validates architecture courses around the world.

In the same year, 1931, that RIBA formalised its education, it also established the Architects' Registration Council of the United Kingdom (ARCUK) to provide statutory registration and regulation for the profession, in order to protect the use of the title 'architect'. This was secured through the Architects (Registration) Act of 1931 (and later revised in 1997). Its function was to prescribe architectural

Figure 1.4 The City of London is fast becoming overwhelmed by skyscrapers, captured in this view from a building that was the highest in London in the seventeenth century, St Paul's Cathedral, built by Sir Christopher Wren. Wren was a notable anatomist, astronomer, geometer and mathematician-physicist, as well as an architect

Source: author.

qualifications, maintain the register of architects and uphold standards of professional conduct and competence (this is not unique to the UK, for example, the Netherlands also has an Architect Registration Office, *Bureau Architectenregister*). However, the relationship between RIBA, which validates the education of architects and promotes architecture, and the ARB, which regulates the profession, has always been uneasy. In 1993, there was a government enquiry into the registration body led by John Warne, a career civil servant and secretary to the Institute of Chartered Accountants. The Warne Report's shocking conclusion was for the abolition of ARCUK. It stated:

> My main recommendation is that the protection of title 'architect' should be abolished and ARCUK disbanded, I believe that this will help modify some of the outmoded distinctions and attitudes which inhibit change within the construction industry. It should also help the efforts being made in the architectural profession to improve the relevance of education and training to the business world in which architects must operate. Although the loss of the monopoly use of the title 'architect' (but not the term 'chartered architect') will be unwelcome to many in the profession, I suggest that time will show that the protection of title has been largely irrelevant to the standing of the architectural profession or to the public interest.[33]

But instead of abolition, RIBA campaigned for a new 'streamlined' registration body because it believed that

> as in other areas of professional service such as law and medicine, consumers of architectural services – and particularly individual one-off consumers – are vulnerable to exploitation with potentially serious consequences for themselves, and for wider consequences for the built environment and society.[34]

So after another consultation process conducted by the Department of the Environment, ARCUK was reconstituted and rebranded as the Architects Registration Board (ARB), but doing almost what it was doing previously. It now operates under the Architects Act 1997. (A similar regulatory body operates in the Netherlands.) Today, each body – RIBA and the ARB – believes the other to be redundant or overlapping with the powers of the other. In 2014, the RIBA council called for an even more streamlined ARB. The ARB's main source of income is fees payable under Part 2 of the Act by persons on their registration or for their retention on the register. Unlike RIBA, which is a membership body, registration with the ARB is compulsory for any architect to practise in the UK. While it is possible to obtain a reduced rate membership fee from RIBA, for the ARB there is no reduction.

In the Building Futures survey carried out by RIBA in 2011 about the future of the profession, surprisingly little was said about its regulatory body. In some countries of the EU, namely Denmark, Finland, Norway and Sweden, there is no national professional body to maintain qualifications and standards. But as can be seen from their architecture, the standards are pretty good and even advanced. There are many countries, especially in the Middle East, where small architectural associations come under the engineering umbrella. It can be said very crudely that RIBA promotes architecture while the ARB is a consumer body. That RIBA promotes architecture and not architects, i.e. it is not a trade union like the British Medical Association (BMA), is a significant difference. So who is promoting architects? Should RIBA be promoting architects (and I do not mean individual architects but as a collective), instead of architecture? How can any form of architectural design survive without architects?

In a report titled 'Collaboration for Change' that was published in 2015, Paul Morrell, the government's former construction advisor, wrote that

> there is a risk that the institutions [can] lose control of the very things that are claimed to differentiate their members from those lacking a professional designation: quality control and oversight of educational standards; a transparent and enforced code of ethics; a defined duty to serve the public interest; the development and dissemination of a relevant body of knowledge; and a demonstration of leadership on some of the great issues that reach across the whole of the built environment.[35]

In 2015, out of the 3,300 RIBA chartered practices, over 2,050 consist of five or fewer people – the proportion of micro-practices is getting larger every year (in 2013, half of the practices had fewer than five people). How RIBA's own aims and aspirations are transmitted down to the small practices' own values will be significant in the continuation of the institute's role.

As a nineteenth-century institute, RIBA faces future demands from the younger generation, and its continued existence is dependent upon its relevance to them. The issue of belonging to any professional organisation for today's emerging architect has been questioned many times. Today, youth culture is more focused on individual aims while connecting virtually on a global scale. They are more of a 'portfolio generation', as Charles Handy would have defined it.[36] Of course the nature of the profession has meant that one can have different responsibilities depending upon the nature of the project – ranging from architect designer, to project manager, to technical designer. Knowledge and research opportunities are available everywhere, so why go to a single organisation? Why not join a virtual organisation that is always available? Architecture is an attractive subject to many younger people, while the idea of belonging to an organisation is not. Rather like religious organisations and edifices, professional organisations are seen as fuddy-duddy. Only time will tell if the organisation that was set up in Victorian times has relevance in the twenty-first century and beyond.

What do architects do all day?

A youthful Thomas Hardy demarcated his daily life of the nineteenth century into three categories: 'the professional life, the scholar's life and the rustic life'. His scholar's life occupied the early hours of 6am to 8am when he studied the Iliad and Aeneid, while his 'rustic life' was spent playing the fiddle, cello or violin with his father or uncle at country dances in the evening. In his professional life fell his work as a draughtsman and later architect. As his fame as an author and poet grew, the 'professional life' of an architect came to an end. But the influence of architecture never left his writings – poems such as 'Copying Architecture in an Old Minster', even pronouncing that 'too regular beat in poetry was bad art', and compositions that carried a Gothic notion of metrical and reversed beats. From his royalties as a novelist, he lived comfortably in a 'big ugly house' he had designed outside Dorchester. Bothered by 'flecks in his eyes', Hardy had always considered that his work as an architect and novelist would support his first love, poetry.[37] While Hardy could live off his architectural designs, however ugly, in order to support his poetry, to do this today would be quite impossible. One way or the other, practising architects have to work. Some work solely in practice,[38] either as the one running the practice (sole practitioner or director) while others work for others (salaried architects).

The architect has been defined rather wordily as

> one who possesses, with due regard to aesthetic as well as practical considerations, adequate skill and knowledge to enable him

> to originate, design, arrange for and to supervise the erection of such buildings, or other works, calling for such a skill in design and planning as he might, in the course of business, reasonably be asked to carry out, or in respect of which he offers his services as a specialist.[39]

The architect's main responsibility in addition to design skills lies as an agent of his or her client. Architects, particularly small practices, have an advantage in being 'direct sellers' who create bespoke designs for their clients. Designer fashion and furniture are popular, even though they might be mass produced, so a bespoke architectural design has even more currency. How such designs are marketed and sold will be of key importance to the small practitioner.

While the domestic residential market is easier to access for small practices, the slowness and the complexity of the UK's procurement system make it harder for small practices to get on to public projects. The EU introduced changes in January 2014 to make procurement easy for SMEs in its procurement directive. But have these changes made it easy for architects to get work? The public contract regulations came into force in February 2015. Clients can now develop as much knowledge as possible about design and construction markets through the Preliminary Market engagement within these new regulations before starting their procurement. It is all very well for a manager in a large construction firm to say, 'We need to educate architects regarding budget, and they need to understand more clearly what the client wants', but how are architects to do this when their fees are being cut?[40] A qualitative approach rather than a tick box approach to writing bids can help SMEs and include factors such as life-cycle costing, community engagement experience, etc. I do believe that architecture as a profession is very fractured (too much competition rather than collaboration) with no external support, and this is perhaps why it has very little influence over government policy, fees, investment, etc. Many small and medium practices are on 'frameworks' for public projects, which allows them to bid for such work. They will have a steady supply of work, but it is difficult for a new practitioner to get on to the framework in the first place. Furthermore, when the work stream from the particular framework sector dies out due to low demand or policy changes, these niche practices may struggle to find other work. In 2013–2014, framework agreements supplied only 10 per cent of new work, and that too for practices with more than 20 people. Some clients now ask practices to bid against each other, driving down fees further.

Low pay and long hours plague the architectural profession whether you are an owner or an employee. Architecture is simply a time-intensive profession despite the extensive use of computer-aided design, CAD and the Internet. We are simply exhausted by what Sir Patrick Bateson calls 'the exhaustion faced by those who face too many demands'.[41]

Architects also have to show that they are keeping on top of professional knowledge, demonstrating at least 35 hours of mandatory continuing professional development (CPD), but usually architects clock up much more than that. Research as part of design work is essential, and learning new digital technologies adds to the complexity of what an architect must know today to practise. The digitalisation of architects' work has also added to the burden of student education. As far as innovation beyond basic research is concerned, a few brave architects are carrying out further research within the studio. Some bigger practices have a separate research arm within the practice, while some do it as part of their work. Practices value research and consider it intrinsic to their work, according to RIBA, which gives out a 'practice-based research' award annually. Apart from technical or functional research during the course of the design or working on competitions, practices are also focusing on areas such as sustainability, design theory, sociology and policy to develop their philosophical approach. As practice-based research is carried out within the studio and without additional resources, this puts an additional burden on small practices (larger practices have more compelling examples of formal research).[42] But architects are so busy running their offices and managing their day-to-day work that time for innovation is scarce and there is resistance to risk-taking.

Politicians and politics are more influential on architecture than we care to recognise. So far there has been only one architect who has been an MP, but that has not improved our status or influence with politicians and local councils, nor our participation in design review panels or other engagement processes. One only has to see the rapid rise of 'Tech City' in Old Street, London, and the skyscrapers in the City of London that have the blessing of the last Mayor of London, to note that politicians can change the look and feel of a city. Institutions have varying degrees of power on the government but they have to compete with others. But the construction industry is being held back by a 'reputation for self interest, an inability

28 Changing world, changing practice

to deliver promised performance and, above all, the fragmentation of the [construction] professions and their unwillingness to voice a coordinated and consistent message'.[43] Although the Homes and Community Agency says that 'architects need to understand why central and local governments do the things they do',[44] it may not be easy to work with the capricious minds of politicians.

Apart from being fickle, politicians and policy-makers do not appear to have an integrated vision of the community. For example, in the rush to build housing (which is benefiting the volume builders more at present), someone has forgotten that people need offices and other community buildings too. So gradually 'buildings with community value' such as pubs, libraries, schools, street markets, etc. are being sold off and demolished for housing, usually exclusive or luxury housing, not social. Taking advantage of loopholes in the planning policies, developers are creating housing schemes that are more like vertical versions of gated communities. Some are being bought as second homes by foreign investors. This is ironic – a 'yes' for housing but a resounding 'no' to community and work. Before housing, there was the rush to build offices and, in a few years' time, once someone discovers that there are no offices left, the office building boom might start again. London, a city based around public and private open spaces and a strong sense of community, is being fractured by such short-sighted policies.[45] Not to mention the dreary sameness appearing everywhere in the streets. Again, perhaps this is not new, as Thomas Hardy observed the same about Victorian developers: 'Window, door; window, door; Every house like the one before.'[46]

Apart from politicians, celebrities are perhaps even more influential. In fact, celebrity land is another route to architecture and design. So if you are anyone famous, you can extend your skills to other things like designing homes and interiors, as seen in the cases of model Kate Moss and actor Brad Pitt. Celebrities also bring up land and building values – again this is not a new phenomenon. The news that Victoria Beckham may move her fashion headquarters in 2016 to West London was welcomed by developers and politicians. She will need more than 40,000 sq feet of offices and studios in the old BBC complex, bringing in jobs and shoppers (and using the services of the construction industry). Since the nearby Westfield Shopping Centre had £1 billion sales in 2014, a rise of 46.5 per cent since its launch, this is viewed as good news for all.

Figure 1.5 An early twentieth-century pub demolished for new housing in West London. According to the BBC, 27 pubs close down every week in the UK due to many reasons such as the availability of cheap alcohol elsewhere. As the pubs close, the land is made available for housing

Source: author.

Figure 1.6 Construction work around the former BBC studios near the Westfield Shopping Centre, Shepherds Bush. These will be turned into 5,000 homes. With starting prices of half a million pounds, these are not affordable. The nearby 100-year-old Shepherds Bush Market is under threat from developers who want to build luxury homes there

Source: author.

The structure of the profession

The structure of the profession is more or less that of small or micropractice studios. In the EU, 74 per cent of practices were one-person practices in 2014 with an average earnings of €29,000. More than one-third were aged under 40, and the number of architects in Europe had increased by 6 per cent from 2012. Significantly the growth is being pushed by the southern European countries due to their higher student numbers. However, whether these architects are finding work is another matter. Only 78 per cent of EU architects are working full time according to the latest figures. Many architects from the EU and outside come to the UK, drawn by the comparatively large numbers of practices, especially in London where more than half are salaried architects. In 2014, 524 architects from the EU were registered in the UK as architects under Europe's arrangements for the mutual recognition of professional qualifications.

But UK practices have found it difficult to fill posts in employment hotspots despite better economic forecasts, according to the RIBA Future Trends survey carried out in 2014. This has a consequent effect on architectural education as well, with students unable to find placements in their year out. According to the Office for National Statistics (ONS), in January 2014, 235 architects were on the dole – only 2.2 per cent of the total registered, but we don't know if all those employed were actually working as architects. UK unemployment rates for architects are relatively low (1.7 per cent according to the January 2014 figures from the ONS), and architects' earnings are relatively high compared with many other industries. So one way or another, architects are doing some work – perhaps thanks to the versatility of the profession.

High-profile practices attract young talent and students. To have a big-name practice on your CV is a global advantage, so new graduates and year-out students vie for work in big-name practices. For the last nine years, Foster + Partners, with a turnover of £153 million (2014 figures), came out as the world's most admired practice in a 2015 survey by *dezeen* magazine[47] – although it is not known on what criteria this was based. It ranked 7 per cent ahead of second-place runners up, Swiss firm Herzog & de Meuron, who took 10 per cent of the vote, while third place was shared by international firm Gensler and the office of Italian architect Renzo Piano. BIG, the firm led by Danish architect Bjarke Ingels, was in fifth position, while sixth place was shared between Oslo- and New York-based Snøhetta, Irish office O'Donnell & Tuomey, New York studios

32 Changing world, changing practice

SHOP Architects and Rafael Viñoly Architects, and global firms KPF and HOK. But apart from the name, what experience and values you take away with you is also important – new graduates may learn more about leadership and business skills in smaller practices than larger ones.

Global practice

According to the 2014 Architects' Council of Europe (ACE) report, the demand for architectural services remains 'muted', with construction output continuing to fall in several key countries. The latest available statistics show that most of the Eurozone is recording no change, or even a decline, in construction output. Most of the growth is limited to countries that are located on the periphery of Europe, for example Eastern Europe. Overall, construction output has been flat for the past five years. Across the EU, the size of the architectural market has fallen by 5 per cent since 2012. However, advances in technology have made it possible for some firms to open offices or establish alliances with other firms in other parts of the world. RIBA has more than 5,000 of its international members based outside the UK, supported by chapters in North America, the Gulf and Hong Kong (as well as India).

Many larger practices are already working in Asia or the Middle East, designing or collaborating in massive urban projects such as cities, airports or infrastructure. The digitalisation of work, including the use of BIM, means that architects can work from anywhere. This makes it possible for some portions of the work to be undertaken in the USA or the UK and other portions in locations such as India or China, for example. In addition to utilising lower-cost, high-skill professionals in Asian countries, it also enables some firms to work, in effect, two or three shifts due to time differences. Global architecture, with the ease of technology and the common aspiration of the Western style of architecture, has become easier and tenable.[48] One-fifth of all British practices are working on overseas projects, with the Middle East being the single most profitable region at present.

But only the largest practices benefit significantly from international work. In the past, Western or Western-educated architects were involved heavily in the building of new capitals and cities in the newly independent countries from the 1940s onwards and tended to be small practices (such as Jane Drew and Maxwell Fry). But now due to the scale of the work, this has become a significant source of work for larger practices. The breadth and scale of the organisational effort required to sustain overseas working is indeed breathtaking. While the news that in 2015 SOM architects created a masterplan for a privately funded new capital city for Egypt might be envy inducing, the organisational support required is beyond the reach of many architectural practices. SOM has now completed over 10,000 projects across more than 50 countries. It has a staff of over 1,000 professionals, working from ten global offices placed in various cities across the continents. This kind of resourcing is not possible for the small practice.

On the other hand, increasingly developers in India and China are hiring smaller US and European firms to work on local developments. These are often coordinated or sub-contracted by architecture firms in these countries – in effect outsourcing work to US and European firms. The market situation has led to an acceleration in this trend, and a growing number of architecture firms in India and China are now outsourcing work to architects in the West. In particular, cultural and environmental contexts should be of prime importance, but built spaces are now developing with no tangible connection to its geographical siting due to the phenomenon of global architecture. The simple transference of styles or materials should not be in itself the goal for the autotelic architect. According to Michael Jenson, global practice needs

> to move beyond interpreting and deploying architectural expertise solely in stylistic or material terms and to begin to comprehend its potential to be an agency for social and cultural transformation within globalisation. To this end, the operative agency of the architect throughout the entirety of the design process from the institutional to the grass roots level needs to be critically re-thought.[49]

The cost of practising architecture

There are 35,000 architects in the UK, very similar to the numbers in China, and yet, due to population differences, we find that in China there is one architect per 40,000 people and, in the UK, 1 per 2,000 people.[50] Italy, which produces more architects than any other EU country, has 2.5 architects per 1,000 people. Chile has one architect per 667 inhabitants, and Mexico has about 724 inhabitants per architect – more even than Italy. According to ACE, the architects from the

Figure 1.7 Modern architecture travelled around the world regardless of context, climate and society in the 1950s. Here is the panorama of the city of Caracas, Venezuela, that is home to many modernist and post-modern buildings built on oil wealth but slowly decaying now due to economic downturn

Source: author.

Changing world, changing practice 35

countries of Eastern Europe report a greater job satisfaction. There we find one architect per 3,000 persons, and so one wonders: does having less architects result in more work and therefore more work satisfaction and better pay? The distribution of architects is another issue, with many architects based in the capital city of the country, making for an uneven distribution. Although RIBA dropped the reference to London in its title nearly 125 years ago, London continues to host one-quarter of British practices. Due to low numbers of architects and smaller sizes of practices, they may find it harder to have a voice in the community and in policy-making, while, in the capital, the competition may be hard on smaller practices. The less architectural discourse, the less the incentive to engage and pay an architect – thus regional offices suffer more than London-based practices. A well-known large practice even closed its regional office in Birmingham (UK's second largest city) because work in the commercial sector was not forthcoming there.

Table 1.1 Architects' salaries and the cost of living index

Country	Average annual architects' salaries (in £)	Cost of living index (CPI) 2014
United Kingdom	34,000	115
United States of America	56,000	100
Rwanda	1,452	60
India	4,200	31
France	22,860	113
China	30,000	57
Brazil	26,000	74
Nigeria	1,200	72
Germany	30,000	82
Spain	24,000	78
United Arab Emirates	7,266	62
Norway	44,000	143
Australia	44,000	116
Japan	32,000	101
Mexico	14,000	52

Note: this table was compiled from various sources – web, anecdotal and research reports. In each country, 'Western-educated architects' earned well above the national average, and expats earned even more. I have listed the salaries of a 'locally educated senior architect'. Again, bigger cities offered more, so, for example, one could earn more in Tokyo than elsewhere in Japan, so I have used the CPI available for the capital cities. Data from the International Labour Organization shows the average worker in the UK earning around £26,100 per year (from www.bbc.co.uk/news/world-31110113, accessed February 2015).

Sources: information from RIBA, Salary Explorer, Archinect, http://salaries.archinect.com/poll/results/country/view-all, accessed September 2014; www.archdaily.com/438093/how-much-do-architects-earn-around-the-world, accessed September 2014; www.numbeo.com, accessed September 2014; and http://thejobseconomist.blogspot.co.uk, accessed September 2014).

36 Changing world, changing practice

The average salary of a mid-ranking architect is £34,000 in the UK, and the salaries of architects around the world show a similar pattern in comparison to the cost of living. Sole practitioners who constitute 14 per cent of UK practices remain the group with the least income (similar to the incomes of fine artists according to a survey in 2008[51]) – with the lowest income once being reported as £5,000 per year.

Although architects may well earn above the national average in many countries, the elephants in the room are the costs of running a practice, such as professional indemnity insurance, training (CPD), overheads and salaries. Bad or sloppy employment practice may be a result of low income and not enough time. In December 2015, RIBA revealed that many practices based in London were moving to the North because of the expense of working in London. Many existing office spaces are being converted to homes, thereby leading to a space shortage for smaller offices. RIBA has opened its 'incubator space' for young practices in central London. At a very small cost, it offers a prestigious address and all the regular accroutrements of offices, such as wi-fi, a café and also free access to CPD events. It offers the possibility of collaborative working, as two of the practices working there told me. However, this is only in London and benefits only one or two main practices, but we will need many more such spaces in other regions.

As can be seen from the cost of living index, though one may earn more in a country such as Norway, the cost of living is high. The financial risks of running an architectural practice, even a big global practice, may be higher. The ARB annual retention fee is now £107 per annum (in 2015) – that represents more than 0.25 per cent of an architect's median earnings. In 2014, 2,000 architects were struck off by the ARB for late payment of fees. RIBA's own fee for chartered practices is now nearly £400. So for the huge numbers of sole practitioners, the cost of being able to run a chartered architectural practice is £500, even without the insurance costs. Being a member of RIBA has advantages but, at present, this is a huge financial burden and may account for the falling numbers of chartered practices that are run by sole practitioners.

Architects are also vulnerable owing to legal actions by others. It is not uncommon to see advertisements that say, 'If you've been let down by [an] architect, we can help', and the advertiser then assures the reader: 'I won't stop until I get the right result for you.' Bad credit is also a problem. Often even bigger practices may be unable to pay their employees because they are owed money by clients and do not have bridging finances. RIBA's second Benchmarking survey advises that practices need to have no more than a 40 per cent stake in any one type of work. Otherwise by putting all their eggs in one basket, they are risking a complete breakdown of the practice.

Salaries also differ according to the size and location of the practice. Partners and directors earn an average of £50,000 – rising to £100,000 in practices with more than 50 staff. But in practices with fewer than five people, partners and directors earn less than £25,000. Private corporate clients account for more than 40 per cent of all the income generated by practices. One-fifth comes from the public sector and one-fifth from contractors. The domestic market accounts for 13 per cent. Within the employment market, there has been a move towards 'salary transparency' in order to remove discrimination, especially for women and Black, Asian and Minority Ethnic (BAME) employees. In the USA, increasing numbers of people review salaries before joining firms. Struggling small British architectural firms might not like to reveal that many owners take pay cuts or no pay in order to maintain salaried staff. On the other hand, some bigger practices have been accused of not paying students. In the end, the solution lies in making architecture a better-paid profession than it is, rather than cutting slices off an ever-shrinking cake.

Equality and diversity in architectural practice

Diversity in the workforce has been shown to be a key driver in understanding markets and client bases as well as boosting innovation.[52] It was only in 1898 that a woman, Ethel Charles (later to be followed by her sister), was 'accepted' as a member of RIBA but, after her victory, she did not stay in the limelight, working on small projects and houses – no doubt due to the general discrimination around in those days. Across the EU, women constitute 39 per cent of architects. About 30 per cent of the UK architectural workforce are female (and not all of them are architects) and their position falls with seniority. Nearly half of architectural assistants are women but only 13 per cent of partners and directors are women. A study found that although the number of female architects rose by 1.7 per cent between 2013–2014 and 2014–2015, the rise was outstripped by a 9.9 per cent rise in the number of male architects.[53]

38 Changing world, changing practice

In 1985, the Salaried Architects Group at RIBA started an off-shoot that became the Women's Architects Group and was later renamed Women in Architecture. This group has campaigned to highlight the inequalities between men and women in architecture through seminars, exhibitions and talks. RIBA's equality forum, Architects for Change, was set up in 2000. Since then, RIBA has elected its first female president in 2009, followed by two other female presidents and also a president from a BAME background. The struggle to recognise female architects continues. For instance, the 'Creative United Kingdom' passport, unveiled in 2015, included portraits of many creative personalities from past and present, including the architect Giles Gilbert Scott, but they were all male. After a successful campaign to have more women, Elisabeth Scott, the 'girl architect' of the Royal Shakespeare Theatre in Stratford-upon-Avon, was one of the two women included in the notes.

The number of BAME building professionals fell by 9.4 per cent in 2013–2014.[54] Included in that group were architects, town planning officers, architectural and planning technicians, consisting of 9,000 from BAME background as opposed to 133,000 white members. Ethnic groups make 8 per cent of the UK's population but only 1.8 per cent of architects.[55] The report said: 'White men are not the only people to use buildings – so diversifying architecture could allow companies to understand new markets and move ahead of the competition.' Interestingly, the report suggested that the lack of BAME architects could be due to the cost of architectural training, rather than discrimination. A 2005 CABE study also did not find any specific reasons for the lack of BAME students and architects; instead there was a combination of factors including cost of study and practice, lack of role models, etc. Unless the cost of studying architecture is reduced for all, it will fail to attract people from diverse backgrounds.

Key drivers of change: faster, less and more

In 2008, Arup published a report listing key drivers of change[56] – water [shortage], climate change, demographics, waste, energy and urbanisation. Each of these are significant factors of change, but I would like to summarise it simply – basically we have to do more with less, faster. Our need to do things quickly has given rise to many innovations, such as technology, the Internet and transport. While the

Changing world, changing practice   39

'more with less, faster' approach has alleviated many problems, it has also been responsible for some unintended consequences. Driving the 'more' aspect has been the exponential rise of the world population and their needs. From the 1960s onwards, there has been seemingly a rapid devolution of power and increase in personal autonomy. We can now question our wars, demand freedom of expression and campaign to remove structural inequalities in society. Change in all aspects of our lives from the end of the twentieth century to the beginning of the twenty-first century and shifts in power have been big, sharp and swift. But we have finite resources, such as clean water and energy.

Under the category of 'more' come both waste and urbanisation because these are on the rise. In the early twentieth century, newly designed cities and buildings of the West were of low density, designed to make use of the health benefits of daylight, ventilation, the outdoors and sunlight. Outdoor public spaces and private spaces were used in the influential garden city concept proposed in Victorian times. Many philanthropic developments such as Port Sunlight, Saltaire and others were built in the hope that design would solve social problems. Later colonial cities such as New Delhi were also modelled on such principles – but with vast green lawns roasting under a tropical sun. But now rapid and universal urbanisation and the increase in car use have given rise to civic problems, pollution and waste in those previously salubrious cities. Over seven million people annually die from air population all over the world. The formation of 'mega cities' has vastly multiplied the scale of the problems of waste and pollution. Of the world's 20 most polluted cities, 13 lie in India – many of these being mega cities as well – and New Delhi is now the world's most polluted city. Such seemingly intractable and connected problems require vast and interlocking solutions, solutions that may be more scientifically or technically inclined – and those that might seem beyond the capabilities of an architect.

It has been said that if the population levels were to go down to 1950 levels, so would all our problems of pollution, crowded cities, lack of water and sanitation, etc., become manageable or even disappear. Prince Charles warned us of the 'terrifying prospect' of an additional three billion people sharing the planet by 2050. 'Architects and urban designers have an enormous role to play in responding to this challenge,' he writes. 'We have to work out how we will create resilient, truly sustainable and human-scale urban environments that are land-efficient, use low-carbon materials and do not depend so completely upon the car.'[57] But the construction

40 Changing world, changing practice

industry has not been consistently supported by the politicians over its 'green' goals. Green subsidies for energy firms have been cut while the government says that it remains committed to the strong global climate change deal signed at the Paris climate change summit in 2015.[58] Energy-saving materials no longer qualify for reduced-rate VAT. (The Building Services Research and Information Association says that it is disappointed that the carbon reduction industry was singled out to be charged the standard rate of VAT.) In the case of the retrofit of existing buildings, enthusiasm was limited and short lived – the government's once 'flagship' Green Deal policy collapsed in July 2015.

Furthermore, the global population is shifting, searching for security – in every sense. It has been said that the refugees from the Middle East are fleeing not only from war but also from climate change. And the reason we have climate change is because we are burning more and more fossil fuels to cater for our increasing population and their needs. 'Green power' as yet does not make up our full demands, so coal-fired stations are still needed. The debacle of Japan's Fukushima power plant has placed serious doubts on the safety of nuclear power stations and Germany has announced its plans to close nuclear power stations. The concept of 'value engineering', mass-produced cheap goods and placed obsolescence within goods and software lead us to discard mountains of computers, phones and even ships in poorer countries where they are dismantled and recycled in dangerous circumstances. Our oceans are choking from garbage. We are literally wasting away our future.

Change in all aspects of our lives from the end of the twentieth century to the beginning of the twenty-first century and shifts in power have been big, sharp and swift. The demand to do things faster has been led and aided by the development of technology, particularly the digital revolution. A report published in 2016 says that along with 'smart cities', super-skyscrapers, underwater bubble cities, 3D homes, furniture and even food that can be downloaded and printed at home will be available in 100 years.[59] While the Internet was initially heralded as an open and democratic space for self-expression and collaboration, it is now controlled by both corporate and state surveillance (GCHQ) and from darker agencies of crime and terrorism. Services on the Internet may be 'free' at the 'point of use', but every digital interaction leads to less freedom and more scrutiny. Here we face a strange dilemma – while the Internet

Changing world, changing practice   41

exhorts us to do things faster, we really cannot because we depend on our ever-shrinking resources, including time. And grappling with the demands of a world seen through a virtual lens is a dangerous adventure in a decentralised world. On the other hand, technology and sustainable solutions could come together for an optimistic future, described in the book *Fourth Industrial Revolution*.[60]

Climate change will have a drastic effect on our built environment, the health and well-being of people and on the natural flora and fauna. The three main impacts of climate change are erratic climate and weather extremes; altered ecosystems and habitats; and risks to human health and society, including their habitat. The UN's Development Programme has warned of the intersecting dangers of climate change and displacement. Despite data suggesting that the rate of increase has slowed, levels of carbon dioxide in the atmosphere – a prime cause of global warming – are higher today than they have been for more than 800,000 years. It will mean more flooding, with more storms, heavier rains and higher winds. Vast engineering solutions will have to be thought of to cope with these problems.

Floods and hurricanes in the West have shown that climate change affects us all – wind and water require no visas. Even in the relative calm and comfort of a rich nation such as the UK, the flood risk map is revised every time there is flooding, as more people and property come under risk. PricewaterhouseCoopers estimates that the damage caused is between £400 million and £500 million, with the insurance industry paying out between £250 million and £325 million. This is already more than twice as much as the economic cost of the 2009 floods. According to Robert Barker, 'it seems strange that we can have technological solutions to protect from fire or reduce emissions [but not for water and flooding]'.[61]

Weather will also become warmer. In June 2009, a UK Climate Projections briefing report predicted that mean annual temperatures would rise by 2°C to 5°C by 2080, based on a 'medium emissions scenario'. It also estimated a sea-level rise of between 13cm and 76cm for the UK by 2095, leading to flooding in areas near the sea, and 'extreme high sea-level events' caused by storm swells could increase to even 1,800 times. Increased temperatures will mean a rise in heat-related mortality of 70 per cent of the population (which is ageing in any case) by the 2020s, according to the Health Protection Agency. More than 52,000 Europeans, mostly elderly, died from heatwaves

Figure 1.8 The roof of a house collapses in a busy shopping street, West London, after Storm Desmond in 2015. The storm was attributed partly to climate change. The severity, suddenness and unpredictability of storms and flooding all point to a chaotic weather system. This unpredictability makes designing buildings a particularly difficult challenge

Source: author.

during the summer of 2003, making the heatwave 'one of the deadliest climate-related disasters in Western history', according to the Earth Policy Institute.[62] Italy and France accounted for the largest number, but there were nearly 2,140 deaths in England and Wales. The link between health and climate change was highlighted in August 2015, when the World Health Organization (WHO) hosted the first international conference on health and climate in Geneva, Switzerland. (It was also WHO's first carbon-neutral meeting.) It concluded with a strong warning that 'in the absence of mitigation and adaptation, climate change poses unacceptable risks to health'. We need smarter and bigger solutions than just cooling or heating buildings (which ironically would increase our carbon emissions). This could mean a mass retrofit of existing housing stock, increasing insulation requirements while using heat conservation, etc. This is where architects could be agents of positive change.

The 'less' bit is about lack of resources, whether natural, manmade or infrastructure, and lack of time. The fact is, there is less to go around as we increase in numbers. So what must be done? Every nation would like to be 'progressive', and each nation desires its citizens to live in a better manner, with all the comforts of the modern [read that as Western] world. Europeans reacted with disbelief at refugees entering from Syria – how come they were dressed so well and had mobile phones? That is not surprising at all – what people see as essential, instead of desirable, has changed from even five years ago. I did not use a mobile phone as a university student but, today, my school-going children use iPhones – and even see them as essential. It has become more difficult to ignore the vast inequalities in society – almost one-third of the UK population fell below the official poverty line at some point between 2010 and 2013, compared with 25 per cent of people across the EU. Despite a rise in overall gross domestic products (GDPs), inequalities persist – 50 per cent of the world's wealth is owned by 1 per cent of its population.[63] If we are to create an equitable society, there needs to be a more equitable distribution of wealth and healthcare.

Radical ideas need a mass of people (quorum sensing) to come to a tipping point in order to be accepted by everyone. A rapid mass conversion to a new idea may be a primitive instinct for survival. Climate change may indeed be an example of this type of reaction, as seen in the nearly 200 nations that gathered in Paris for the COP21 summit in 2015. According to a leading sociologist, fear also plays a key role in our collective decision-making. But on a positive note, collective

Figure 1.9 Spikes to deter the homeless in central London. A group of 21 charities called for a drive to end the growing homelessness on London's streets. The average homeless person dies aged just 47 – 30 years younger than the national average – and is 13 times more likely to be a victim of violence. More than 7,500 people slept rough in London last year, including 880 under-25s, and research shows the figure has almost doubled in six years

Source: author.

decision-making can also be affected by interaction, i.e. people influencing each other, and by going on to collaborate and become even more powerful. Ideas that are the most influential often come from the ground up – between public opinion and institutional power, it is the former driving the latter. Perhaps we should now accept that designer and architect will return to their original position of being part of an overall change, but not leading it. As designing is about planning for change, architects will need to collaborate more with health professionals, psychologists, engineers, surveyors, scientists and even politicians to change our world for the better. The circular economy, cradle to grave (or even cradle to cradle) life-cycle assessment and corporate social responsibility has been given a crucial imperative to change a world where greed, anger and ignorance prevailed (and still do).[64]

Architecture is part of the construction industry, which is expected to grow by 23 per cent over the next two years, contributing £12 billion to the UK economy. The construction industry is a barometer of the economy – building has always been with the money right from the days of the Pyramids. Paul Morrell wrote: 'It is one of the conclusions of the Commission [for Change (2015)] that the threats and pressures for change that the [construction] professions [including architecture] face, if not yet existential, are real and profound, and demand change.'[65] But we architects might be more resilient than we think and our knowledge base is impressive. For one, consider that the study of architecture is also an extensive study, ranging from history, geography, economics and law, as well as elements of construction, surveying and engineering. We are actually better placed than many of our co-professionals to adapt to the requirements of 'faster, more or less'. Adrian Dobson, Practice Director at RIBA,[66] believes that it is in the expansion of skills, and not specialisation, that the work of the architect will survive. He also says that architects need to be politically engaged and astute – looking out for opportunities, and not wait for them.

The Georgian and Victorian times in the UK were also times of great upheaval. In fact the concept of 'doing more with less, faster' arose as part of the Industrial Revolution. Holding fast to an unfailing belief in human endeavour, technology and 'progress', these people sailed in treacherous seas to find and exploit new lands, came back with exotic produce that they would refine and reuse (and export), dug tunnels under rivers or bridged them with daring engineering, conquered distances by designing faster trains (and even prototype planes) and built many kinds of experimental buildings using new technology, such as

46 Changing world, changing practice

the Crystal Palace. Even the Queen took an interest in the technology, visiting the Great Exhibition five times and spending over 50 hours there, with its displays and products chosen by the people. Anybody with an interest and inclination could do anything – a vet could invent pneumatic tyres, an illiterate farmhand could design fairground technology and an Earl could invent a special hat (the Bowler) to protect his gardener from injury. If a Victorian were to come back today, he or she would relate to pretty much everything except the technology we use. Of course, a lot of this was funded by imperialistic exploits and used without any regard for the environment or ethics. Thousands died in Victorian ventures, and large swathes of land and water were polluted. Looking at the hills of discarded glass bottles left by the Victorians in the Heligan estates in Cornwall, I could not help thinking that, with regard to ethics and ecology, we cannot go back to Victorian times. But regarding having the spirit to help humanity from the consequences of Georgian and Victorian revolutions, we might learn to have a similar daring and spirit. Mihaly Csikszentmihalyi, Professor of Psychology and Management, who devised the theory of 'flow', says:

> [Autotelic persons] are more autonomous and independent because they cannot be as easily manipulated with threats or rewards from the outside. At the same time, they are more involved with everything around them because they are fully immersed in the current of life.[67]

It may be just the right time for an autotelic architect.

Notes

1 Gombrich (1984, p. 4).
2 Ibid., p. 18.
3 Ibid., p. 19.
4 Wilson (2011, pp. 12–23).
5 Wigglesworth and Till (1998, p. 74).
6 'Island life diversifies', *RIBAJ*, September 2014, p. 76.
7 www.bdonline.co.uk/5081341.article?origin=BDdaily (accessed May 2016).
8 98 per cent according to some, including the *Guardian*.
9 Reproduced in 'The AA story', 1936–39, *FOCUS*, 4, 1939.
10 Ian Youngs, 'Is it art?', www.bbc.co.uk/news/entertainment-arts-35034834 (accessed December 2015).
11 'What do developers want from architects?', *RIBAJ*, May 2015, p. 51.
12 www.lettersofnote.com/2010/03/advice-for-an-aspiring-architect-in-1931.html (accessed September 2011). Emphasis added.
13 Ibid.
14 John Soane, from the introduction to *Plans, Elevations and Sections of Buildings* (1971). Emphasis added.

Changing world, changing practice 47

15 http://ad009cdnb.archdaily.net/wp-content/uploads/2013/02/511bb6b fb3fc4b42d200003b_the-100-largest-architecture-firms-in-the-world_ where-the-worlds-100-post_04_retina_02.jpg (accessed December 2014). AECOM's swelling numbers are reportedly due to the Rio Olympics in 2016 but now, in 2016, Gensler has moved back to No. 1.
16 Ibid.
17 No information was available about South America or Africa.
18 SMEs earn less than €50 million and have less than 250 employees.
19 BD online, 17 September 2015; a reader comments: 'All architects do is enjoy canapés and five-hour liquid lunches with the client, then repair to their Barbican duplex to write comments on BD Online about what a hard life it is being an impoverished architect.' www.bdonline. co.uk/news/stirling-prize-ceremony-targeted-by-social-housing-activists/5077855.article (accessed October 2015).
20 *Building Design*, 10 June 2015. http://www.bdonline.co.uk/news/ bartlett-dean-warns-developers-are-in-danger-of-repeating-mistakes-of-1960s/5075880.article (accessed June 2015).
21 Michael Benedikt, 'Less for less yet', *Harvard Design Magazine*, 1999.
22 BD online, 16 September 2014. www.bdonline.co.uk/news/ patrik-schumacher-britains-supremacy-at-risk-because-students-shun-maths/5070888.article (accessed September 2014).
23 www.abc.es/cultura/20141023/abci-gehry-peineta-oviedo-principeasturias-201410231845.html (accessed June 2014).
24 'The Architect and his Office: A survey of organization, staffing, quality of service and productivity', presented to the RIBA Council on 6 February 1962, London.
25 Scott (1985, p. ix).
26 'Investment strategy', *RIBAJ*, February 2014, p. 46.
27 'Will Alsopp rebooted', *RIBAJ*, January 2015, p. 48.
28 www.bdonline.co.uk/news/run-more-competitions-riba-tells-clients/ 5071366.article (accessed October 2014).
29 Personal communication.
30 www.architecture.com/Files/RIBAProfessionalServices/CompetitionsOffice/ CompetitionsTaskGroupReport.pdf (accessed December 2014).
31 'Ancient Egypt: The Story of Life and Death', BBC, first broadcast in March 2013.
32 RIBA Royal Charter 1934.
33 Warne Report, 'Review of the Architects (Registration) Acts 1931–1969', ARB, 1997.
34 RIBA's submission to the Call for Evidence on Architects Regulation and the Architects Registration Board, 29 May 2014, presented to the Council, p. 3.
35 www.edgedebate.com/wp-content/uploads/2015/05/150415_collaboration-forchange_book.pdf (accessed September 2014).
36 Handy (1995).
37 Wright (1978, p. 14).
38 There are 6.8 million lone workers, including the self-employed, according to an ONS survey in 2015. According to the Royal Society of Arts (RSA), the numbers of self-employed will overtake those in the public

48 Changing world, changing practice

sector by 2018. For many, the loss of security is offset by the ability to look after children.

39 Scott (1985, p. 9). *R v Architects' Registration Tribunal*. Ex parte Jaggar 1945 citing the adopted test of the ARCUK.
40 'It's all about the knowledge', *RIBAJ*, December 2014, p. 35.
41 Bateson, Patrick, 'Playfulness', *CAM magazine*, issue 71, p. 37, 2014.
42 'How practices use research', RIBA, January 2015.
43 'Home truths from a thriving sector', *RIBAJ*, September 2014, p. 49.
44 Ibid., p. 51.
45 www.bdonline.co.uk/news/architects-stage-protest-against-housing-and-planning-bill/5079469.article (accessed January 2016).
46 Wright (1978, p. 171).
47 www.dezeen.com/2015/01/09/foster-partners-worlds-most-admired-architect-ninth-year-in-a-row (accessed September 2015).
48 Jenson (2014).
49 Ibid.
50 www.archdaily.com/501477/does-italy-have-way-too-many-architects-the-ratio-of-architects-to-inhabitants-around-the-world (accessed November 2015).
51 www.thisismoney.co.uk/money/news/article-1618829/The-best--worst-paid-jobs-Britain.html (accessed December 2015).
52 www.nytimes.com/2015/12/09/opinion/diversity-makes-you-brighter.html?ribbon-ad-idx=26&rref=homepage&module=Ribbon&version=o rigin&region=Header&action=click&contentCollection=Home+Page& pgtype=article&_r=0 (accessed December 2015).
53 'Women in architecture survey', *Architects' Journal*, 30 September 2015.
54 Report into the creative industries produced by the Creative Industries Federation, in partnership with Music of Black Origin. 'Number of black and ethnic minority architects drops', *AJ*, 30 September 2015.
55 'Making a difference', *RIBAJ*, February 2014, p. 63.
56 Dr Chris Luebkeman, 'Key drivers of change', Arup, 2008.
57 HRH The Prince of Wales, 'Viewpoints', *Architectural Review*, 20 December 2014.
58 www.ft.com/cms/s/0/96ec7b9c-7648-11e5-933d-efcdc3c11c89.html# axzz3t6nTp5vS (accessed November 2015).
59 www.samsung.com/uk/pdf/smartthings/future-living-report.pdf (accessed April 2016).
60 Rifkin (2013).
61 www.bdonline.co.uk/comment/opinion/flood-proof?-designing-against-the-tide/5077475.article (accessed September 2015).
62 www.bbc.co.uk/news/magazine-35037983 (accessed December 2015).
63 www.theguardian.com/business/2015/jan/19/global-wealth-oxfam-inequality-davos-economic-summit-switzerland (accessed January 2015).
64 Braungart and McDonough (2009).
65 www.edgedebate.com/wp-content/uploads/2015/05/150415_collaboration forchange_book.pdf (accessed September 2014).
66 Interview: 16 September 2014.
67 Csikszentmihalyi (1997, p. 17).

2 Practice of architecture

When John Soane came back from his grand tour of Europe in 1780, he was £120 in debt – a massive sum in those days.[1] But he had made contact with other artists, actors, singers and architects, watched the opera, sketched, made plans for possible projects and learnt Italian. Coming from a humble family of bricklayers, these contacts and experiences would make a huge difference to his later life. Anxious to find work, he hurried to Suffolk where he thought he would get a commission to build for the Earl of Bristol and pay back his debts. He was after all 27 years old, which in those days was rather late to start working. But the Earl had changed his mind and sent him to Londonderry where there were plans to rebuild another house. They then had a disagreement over the design and Soane was not commissioned, leaving with just £30 for his efforts. He then sailed to Glasgow for a possible project for someone he had met in Rome, but that also came to nothing. He returned to London where some of his newly made friends took pity on him and found him some minor commissions such as building renovations. But he was hoping for grander work, a chance to show off his talents. George Dance, the architect, who had employed him as a teenager, gave him some small projects, including works to a prison. He then entered a competition to design a prison but failed to win. During this time, he continued to get only minor commissions, such as renovations, design of gates and small farm buildings.

Three years later, at the age of 30, Soane's perseverance paid off and he received his first commission for a country house in Norfolk. He continued to receive such work until his retirement when he was nearly 80 years old. His biggest work, the Bank of England, was constructed when he was just 35, and it was also the result of contacts made during his Italian travels. Though inexperienced, he was to make a shrewd business decision. He asked to receive 5 per cent of

50 Practice of architecture

the budget of any building works, which might seem a bit modest. But he exploited this arrangement to the maximum – by virtually rebuilding every bit and extending the building as much as he could in its 3½ acre site. In his 45 years there, this commission sustained him, brought him further work and established his name. But between 1925 and 1939, Herbert Baker demolished Soane's three-storeyed building, creating a new building that was seven storeys above ground and three below, to accommodate the increasing volume of work and employees in the bank. Nikolaus Pevsner has described this as 'the greatest architectural crime, in the City of London, of the twentieth century'.[2] Now, of course, Baker's work is dwarfed by the skyscrapers being built in the vicinity.

Soane's story is not atypical of an autotelic approach to life. His resilient wait for work while working on small jobs, making useful contacts and biding his time until he secured his dream project – and then his cleverness in using his biggest commission to create more work and income for himself – hold useful lessons for us today. And that of his usurper, Sir Herbert Baker, also is a significant story. Baker would go on to have an international profile, working on colonial buildings around the world. He would make it a career to outshine other architects, using buildings. His Houses of Parliament in New Delhi, for instance, sited cleverly, hide the grandeur of Edwin Lutyen's Presidential Palace behind it in an architectural coup called 'Bakerloo' by Lutyens. But perhaps the most important lesson here is to remember that context is always changing and that the nature of architecture is really ephemeral. Autotelic architects take advantage of whatever life throws at them. Life in Soane's or Baker's time was also hard and yet they created opportunities where none existed.

Wishing to learn how creative people could be business-like too, during 2015 I organised four 'creative soirées' that brought together creative people (artists, architects, writers, film makers, photographers and designers) as well as business people in discussions about how to be creative as well as commercial. Wishing to widen the debate, I shared our discussions on social media, which invited further comments. I also interviewed a number of architects separately about work practice. We discussed what successful architects and other creative people had to say about running a successful practice. Some of the participants and commentators came from big architectural practices, some from smaller practices or some were sole practitioners.

The business of practising architecture is not like other professions. Architecture has always offered the possibility of flexible working

Figure 2.1 New architecture dominates the area around the old Bank of England. What would Soane or even Baker have made of this new, high-rise building? A report from New London Architecture and GLHearn published in March 2016 revealed that the total number of proposed tall buildings in London, i.e. buildings of 20 floors or over, is 436

Source: author.

in more ways than one. Professional practice combined with artistic endeavours or teaching has been most common, but there are new ways as well – such as being a consultant or advisor or a developer. Joseph Paxton was an architect, a landscape architect, a director of Midland Railways and an MP – out of these positions, only the successful speculation in the railways offered him continuing financial stability. This kind of work flexibility and choice is hardly seen in other professions. This flexibility also offers an envious retreat into creativity that other professions perhaps would love to have. I know a couple of accountants who have creative pastimes but they do not have the opportunity that architecture offers – that of creativity within their work.

In the architect's case, creativity is central to their work. But that is not all – being a good business person is equally important. How we manage our finances, how we treat our colleagues and employees, how we source our products, how we keep up with research and CPD, how we network, etc. are all part of running a successful business. How architects manage these two seemingly divergent aspects of their work – being both creative and commercially minded – is a continuing preoccupation for the profession. Many other creative endeavours do not have, for example, CPD as an essential requirement, although some level of research is useful for any career.

Getting paid and on time

'Getting paid and on time' was a common theme for all the self-employed people who attended my creative soirées. One of my LinkedIn posts titled 'Why hire an architect when anyone can design for free?' about being paid properly, turned out to be the most popular. Let's look at the profession of law in particular, as a comparison, because many lawyers are self-employed and run their own firms. Lawyers generally charge for every 6 minutes of work they do at an hourly rate (and sometimes a fixed fee). And how much do they spend studying law? According to the Law Society, the overall cost of a law degree could be as much as £26,000 (including living expenses). After finishing, newly qualified lawyers can earn £30,000–40,000. Law is a short course and you can also take up other routes for studying – you can transfer from another course or you can do a short, specialised course after finishing your first degree. Given the relative ease of completing a law course and the starting salaries, it is no wonder that it is the second most popular degree course at UK universities after business and management studies. Now, compare these figures

Practice of architecture 53

to the total costs of studying and registering as an architect – upwards of £88,000 after at least 8–9 years of study, the debt taking many decades to pay off. The starting salaries of an architect range from £26,000–35,000. I do not analyse these figures from a 'sour grapes' point of view but do wonder if society deems our work worthy enough to be paid properly?

It has been said that 'What gets measured, gets managed' or, conversely, 'If you can't measure it, you can't manage it.'[3] However, managing or measuring your time alone may not ensure you get paid. Our penchant for the bottomless pit of precision and perfection, the fear of litigation and, sometimes, the simple need for that creative time, make us time-intensive professionals. We are poor time keepers because of our creative urges – one small task can engross us for hours. Our studies are also time intensive as well. So our low pay arises from the disproportionately longer time spent on a particular piece of work. Say an architect is paid £80 for a drawing and spends three hours on it – after tax, that might come to only £10. In contrast, if a lawyer is paid £80 for a piece of work, it might be actually one hour's worth of work and therefore after tax will be £64. While I can see that there is no way to decrease this creative time (and indeed our clients would be unhappy if we did), I wondered if there were other ways of increasing our fees in a manner that clients would accept?

According to the latest surveys, architects in the EU get paid in four main ways:

- a percentage of the total build cost – 47 per cent;
- a lump sum payment – 32 per cent;
- an hourly rate – 14 per cent;
- a flexible amount – 7 per cent.

The percentage fee is the most popular with France leading here, while in Sweden and Finland, hourly and lump sum payments were more popular. In the UK, the percentage method was used by 31 per cent of practices, the lump sum by 45 per cent and the hourly charge by 21 per cent. Some small architectural practices insist on getting paid by the hour, especially for smaller residential projects, which are notorious for clients changing their minds and the excruciating negotiations about party walls and other matters that take up the time. Across the EU in 2015, earnings have not gone up since 2012 – the average salary for architects remains around €29,000. Architects in Italy, Ireland, Portugal and Spain also remain dissatisfied with their career choice, primarily because of the income it generates.

54 Practice of architecture

In 2015, there were shockwaves after an award-winning small architectural practice went out of business with less than £270 in their business account. Low fees, too much speculative work and a lack of big projects were cited by the practice for their financial problems. In my own review of architecture, poor pay came up as a constant hindrance for architects. A small income also impacts on other areas of an architect's practice. The money does not stretch out to cover overheads and, sometimes, not even salaries. Bad employment practices such as avoidance of statutory employment rights, discriminatory practice and ignoring health and safety directives are a result of not having enough time or resources to deal with these issues. The long hours culture has been blamed for the low numbers of female architects and for the 'macho' culture of many practices.[4] While it is good to be pro-active, it is not good to be over active to the detriment of yourself and your practice. I know of an architect who runs or works in three practices. Are we trying too hard? There needs to be a happy medium between negligence and perfection. We ought to be confident about the way that architecture creates value for the world we live in. So how do we mitigate poor pay? One succinct piece of advice comes from Laurie Baker, 'only accept a reasonable brief'.[5] This does not mean a limiting of ambition but being realistic of what can be delivered within a budget and time. As an architect advised: 'Don't try and compete on price but on quality. One-man bands and micro-practices cannot deliver consistent high quality on any job larger than a domestic extension'.[6]

One solution could be about managing one's time so that one is paid for the time worked. The 80:20 'Pareto's Law' is a fairly reliable tool for decision-making about time management – 20 per cent of your clients bring in 80 per cent of your income while you may be working 80 per cent of your time for clients who may be bringing just 20 per cent of the work. 'Front end work' such as taking plans up to permission stages produced fees for 87 per cent of practices, feasibility studies 73 per cent and planning advice delivered fees for 50 per cent of architects. Such advice is valued by clients because 'architects can, and do initiate design concepts'.[7] While this trend is likely to strengthen the image of the architect as a nerdy, desk-bound 'concept' designer, not as a muscular practical worker, this is at least an area that our cognate professionals (quantity surveyors and architectural technicians to name two) cannot claim as theirs. But this also may have an effect on the architectural skills and education needed in the future.

However, another thing that takes up time, especially for a small practitioner, is new technology and communications, which ironically are meant to save time. How we manage this is also about making best use of the 80:20 law. According to Cal Newport, there are two kinds of work:

- 'Deep work' is using your skills to create something of value. It takes thought, energy, time and concentration.
- 'Shallow work' is all the little administrative and logistical stuff: email, meetings, calls, expense reports, etc.[8]

Newport recommends spending more time in deep work because it is more productive than in shallow work, although getting through a stack of emails can feel more productive. Plus, answering emails costs time and money. For example, the Chief Technology Officer of Atlantic Media, which publishes *The Atlantic* magazine, wanted to know how much they were paying people just to respond to emails. When he ran the numbers, it turned out that it was about $1 million dollars a year! So, some companies have found innovative ways of dealing with shallow work – Virgin trains staff now use an electronic sorting system that classifies emails based on key words and then forwards them to the relevant person. This may not be possible for a small business but limiting email and social media time can be either limited or outsourced to someone else. Limiting email time works for any company, whatever its size – a social entrepreneur started answering emails once a week and realised he had been more productive than usual.[9]

Diversification of income could be another solution. There are architects who teach or do other things to 'support' their practice (unlike Thomas Hardy, whose architectural practice supported his first love, poetry). Another contrasting technique could be about playing up one's core skills – to do what one can do best and not to diversify. One's practice could be about specialisms, such as housing, healthcare or conservation. In employment, one could hire the best people to make up what one may lack and complementary skills without duplication. So instead of becoming a dilemma, doing what one is most skilled in. Le Corbusier, throughout his career, devoted half of his time to design and the other to art, leaving the office management to others. He would work alone (but the lone genius office organisation is no longer an autotelic way to work, as we will see in Chapter 4). The late Dame Zaha Hadid told me that she spends 90 per cent of her time being creative. On the other hand, I know of a very successful commercial architect who spends most of his time managing his office and getting work while his staff work on projects. Although these are two contrasting approaches, there is a common point – both of these architects do what they can do best and delegate to others the things

56 Practice of architecture

they cannot do or do not have time for. One of them may have the best managers in the office to handle the business side of things and the other may have the best creative brains. Someone's strongest point may be being creative while for someone else that might be management and business skills, not design. Harriet Green, former CEO of the Thomas Cook Group, in a BBC interview said: 'Whatever it is that you are not, surround yourself with them.'[10]

Value-based fees

So can you quantify the value you bring to your project? The *RIBAJ* headlined this dilemma by saying that 'Architects add value to place, society and client's ideas, but getting that point across can be an uphill struggle.'[11] I remember an erstwhile client whose villa I was designing in Spain. After I had done the initial site survey, produced drawings and a model, visited and interviewed potential suppliers and builders (all the time while also looking after a toddler), the client gasped at my audacity when I presented a modest invoice. 'But I could have done all this myself', she protested. 'So why didn't you?' I thought but I didn't say this aloud. I had an okay time in Spain and she had paid for the airfares and put us up, so I did not pursue this. I remain grateful to her because as a young architect then, I had learnt a great lesson about valuing my work and time, which I have never forgotten.

What do other professions do? Accountants in the USA are one step ahead by using 'value billing' and refusing to bill by the hour, which they say worries clients. An accountant based in the USA explains how this works:

> For standard compliance-based services, value billing tends to form more of a menu-based pricing structure, but consultancy and other 'value-added' services are charged according to the value they create to the business. For example, if you were operating as a sole trader earning a fair salary for professional work, I could suggest you incorporate to save National Insurance Contributions [NICs]. If that saving was worth £3,000 annually to you, you may be willing to pay £1,500 in year one for the advice and company paperwork and then £1,000 thereafter because the saving has created a very clear perception of value. However, on a traditional time billing approach you could have paid significantly less because the advice is actually quite standard (not specialist) and the paperwork is done online using software. Of course there will be scenarios that work the other way around. Despite being a relatively young, dynamic and IT literate

accountant, I still favour time billing, but it is getting increasingly difficult to win new work and maintain good open relationships with clients when they are worried about a very loud clock ticking and a timesheet recording every 6 minutes.[12]

An engineer also supported the idea of value pricing for small works:

> The issue of value is of course subjective. When I [consulted] for a small [architectural] practice it was a constant source of frustration that domestic clients would quibble over a bill for a few hundred pounds, because they only got a few pages of paper in return. But would think nothing of spending £10,000 on a bathroom or kitchen. The structural elements are nearly always hidden of course. So the client doesn't see a tangible benefit. As architects you have far more scope for influencing the client, perhaps you should use this to highlight the value that you bring to the project? This brings to mind a fable about a mechanical engineer who was called onto a large steam ship when the engines had stopped working properly. He had a good look at the engine and spent a few minutes listening and watching the pistons. He then got out his hammer and tapped the engine in one particular spot. He charged the ships captain £1,000, which of course the captain disputed. 'But you only hit the engine with a hammer', he said. To which the engineer replied: 'Yes, the fee is £5 for the hammer blow but £995 for knowing where to strike!'[13]

Undervaluing of architecture

So let's come to the meat of the matter – the undervaluing of architecture. In the case of design, why is it just architectural design that is so undervalued? Why is it that people are happy to queue up all night and spent £750 for a phone? Or that they'd rather spend £35,000 on a flashy car but live and work in dismal surroundings? The problem may be that it is difficult to estimate the value of design while we need quantifiable data in order to judge the value of anything. The now defunct CABE published many booklets on the value of design. One of them was called the Value Handbook in 2007, which listed many values – Exchange, Use, Image, Social, Environmental and Cultural. Most of these except the first one did not demonstrate tangible benefits and some of them start on a questionable basis. For example, consider the heading 'Good design increases a project's chances of being a financial success' (p. 12). Many clients would consider that in an age of austerity, being a financial success is in itself an indicator of good design, not the other way round. Value for money is

58 Practice of architecture

the new criteria for all projects – big or small. At a meeting with a client to discuss a large project, one of the directors of the company, looking at me, said: 'Why do we need an architect? I suppose we could just build a cheap shed' (and I don't think he was joking).

The problem with conventional value systems is that they are subjective and the financial rewards bear no relationship to the social value a particular vocation produces. In a YouGov poll of 2011, 74 per cent of respondents stated that 'responsibility' was the prime factor in determining how much one should be paid.[14] But the actual labour market functions differ markedly from this poll. For example, if responsibility was really appreciated, then nurses or teachers would get paid more than bankers. In a similar vein, talking about the social value that architects bring won't make a blind bit of difference to their pay. As an example, Richard Simmons, who was chief executive of CABE from 2004–2011, recounts:

> I recalled Andy Burnham [the then health minister] asking in 2006 for more evidence to justify good design to NHS accountants. This, in spite of CABE and others researching shedloads of data confirming a no brainer: patients benefit from better-designed healthcare buildings.[15]

This kind of enquiry into the usefulness of architecture goes on. Despite the Farrell report on the value of architecture, only published in March 2014, the government launched a parliamentary inquiry into the 'positive effect of design on human behaviour' in June 2015.

RIBA's 'Client and architect: Developing the essential relationship' report was published in September 2015. But even then, none of these explored the customer psychology – all emphasis was the architect. It emphasised that architects need to do marketing, talk about value, carry out post occupancy evaluation, etc. Tellingly, one of the award-winning projects featured in that report had the client talking quite frankly about it in another report published in the *RIBAJ*: 'If our trustees had known what the final bill was going to be on day one they would not have [commissioned] it.'[16] It looks like clients are nervous – they need a lot of reassurance, especially for public projects. The issue is simply this: when there is an economic disincentive involved, consumers tend not to use a service, no matter how much we talk about value they produce. As a project director told me, 'Why do we need architects? They are only after prizes.' RIBA is cautious: 'The value of the product is not what it costs to provide or produce, it is the value the customer puts on it.'[17] How clients value your work is not necessarily how you may value it. So potential clients see the architect's fee as an economic disincentive – not as a future money saver.

As a small practice based in London, Barbara Weiss Architects has been charging for private residential work on an hourly basis, rather than on the traditional percentage one. They say that they came to this method from two important realisations:

> The first, that each client is very different, and has different expectations in terms of the architect's involvement and extent of hand-holding required during the course of the project. While some clients will expect the architect to spend inordinate amounts of time in helping in the choice of materials, or drawing up infinite alternative room proposals, others will know their own mind, or will not be concerned about finessing the very last detail. We did not feel that it would be fair to charge both types of client the same amount. The second, that we, and many of our clients, did not feel comfortable with establishing fee levels that depended on the 'Russian roulette'-style client choice of materials: expensive marble in the bathroom, you are quids in; cheap tiles in the same bathroom, you make a loss. This approach always causes clients to be suspicious of their architect's motives, generating a mutual lack of trust from the start.[18]

Barbara Weiss says that when they charge hourly, they always advise clients that their rates are very low compared to those of other professionals and explain that in the search for quality they inevitably spend many hours on every project, with the result that the total fees end up being high. But they ensure that the clients fully understand fee projections and the scope of work before starting. For projects with a construction cost of above £350,000, they offer to cap fees at 20 per cent, which gives clients a 'worst-case scenario' figure. To make the business sustainable, a businessman advised that architects need to set their clocks more generously (like the lawyer's). Another way of quantifying value could be like this, as proposed by a businessman attending one of the creative soirées. Say you are invited to design something on a brownfield site and, as a result, you find out that the land value will rocket up. That rise is quantifiable and 10 per cent of that is what you should be stating as your fees, instead of 10 per cent of the construction budget as architects normally do. He advised: 'As a designer, you are a participant in the creation of value and, therefore, your fee should be a percentage of that value. You are selling a premium product and that should be your line'.[19] The CIC's Design Quality Indicator is an initiative where architectural design values have been quantified to some extent. However, as with other studies, this misses out on the small residential projects that in the EU, constitutes 53 per cent of an architect's workload (and majority of the British architect's work).[20]

60 Practice of architecture

The tongue factor

Is there a way of making design desirable? Designer Stephen Bayley said: 'You know the design is good if you want to lick it.'[21] We need to work on the premise of creating a 'desire for architecture' instead of producing endless reports and reviews about how great it is. Desire (heart) makes us do things that do not tie with logic (head). Desire makes us jump from safety into the unknown. Desire as a philosophy can be ethically variable – it can be skilful, unskilful or neutral (while greed and lust are always undesirable). The desire for a better way of life, for better work or health, is part of what makes us human. Tsunesaburo Makiguchi, the Japanese philosopher whose ideas have influenced 'branding', had a unique view of value. He saw creative and contributive values as the most immediate and crucial questions of our daily lives. His value system comprised goodness (good for society), beauty and gain (benefit). It is perfectly possible; just look at the way iPhones are promoted – no prices but just how good or cool it looks and its benefits. Perhaps architects need to reframe their services by creating a desire for good design and value. Let us see how other products do this.

Friends or family who give a positive review of a certain product or service will tip the scales in favour of one brand over another – in our case, architectural design over other sorts of design. The NHS uses the 'Friends and Family' test in which the only question is whether the user would recommend that hospital or clinical service to their friends and family. In some markets, the only real difference between products is brand awareness. Pepsi carried out a test in the 1970s and called it the Pepsi Challenge, which proved this theory. Groups of people were asked to report on which drink – Coca-Cola or Pepsi – tasted better in a blind test. People preferred the taste of Pepsi, but when the tasters could see the labels on each sample, they preferred the taste of Coca-Cola instead! This was because Coca-Cola had created stronger brand awareness.

A successful brand awareness campaign may also encourage repeat purchases and, thus, create a sustainable business. Like the iPhone that almost everyone carries, the house you live in (or your client's house that you designed) can be the best advertisement for good housing. You may have watched 'The House that 100K Built' on the BBC – a valiant attempt by architects Kieran Long and Piers Taylor to get self-builders to understand that good design does not need huge amounts of money, as usually feared. They did this by taking these self-builders to see well-designed homes (usually architects' own homes), which created a desire in them for well-designed homes. This was then broadcast that on national TV. To use a car analogy,

Figure 2.2 The first iMac. Steve Jobs introduced this computer in June 1998 by just describing its benefits, including beauty. 'The back of our computer,' he said, 'looks better than the front of the other guys. It looks like it's from another planet. A good planet. A planet with better designers.' People had never seen a computer that looked like this, yet this product saved Apple computers and made them market leaders

Source: author.

62   Practice of architecture

designing cars for customers' dreams put General Motors on top of the utilitarian Ford Model T. GM designed cars that played on the fantasy of driving a vehicle that feeds your status, imagination and pleasure. That sort of appeal to consumers' hearts as well as wallets is almost entirely missing from the mass housing market.[22]

Various subconscious cues such as incentives, peer pressure, avoidance of loss and societal norms shape our choices – generally we like things that make us feel better.[23] So, although difficult, changing the hearts and minds can be achieved. Professor Joel Robbins gives the example of the Urapmin people in Papua New Guinea who suddenly converted to Christianity in 1977. They said that they had converted after an encounter with the Holy Spirit. However, the truth may have been more pragmatic. While others prospered, the Urapmin had lost their status. But after converting, they regained their status and thrived. Professor Robbins believes that an instinctive need to get their status back converted the Urapmin.[24]

For the architectural profession, the need to get our status back and prosper may act like an incentive to practise the autotelic way and change our institutional structures. Before the iPhone usurped the market with its disruptive new design, people did not know how a mobile phone could be so different. Now every mobile phone wants to look like an iPhone. When the first Modernist buildings appeared without ornamentation, it must have been a shock. Gradually we have become used to it and now many of these buildings are lovingly preserved for posterity. But those buildings came in the crest of a popular culture that included social and lifestyle changes – therefore more acceptable (and autotelic). Acceptance comes with social acceptance in a critical mass of people, so architects would have to become adept at recognising social changes and presenting small 'shocks' rather than big changes, which the public may dismiss immediately.

But then persuading your client to dish out the right amount of fees for your design work needs some additional work – hard cash needs hard data. The post-occupancy evaluation of successful projects may be used to win more work by highlighting both desirable characteristics and tangible benefits. A practice that designed the offices of the National Grid was able to demonstrate that the new offices saw a 5 per cent increase in collaborative working, a 5 per cent time saving, a saving of £8–10 million from not moving offices, a productivity boost of £20 million

Figure 2.3 Private house in Ealing, London, converted from an ordinary, two-storey house to look like the Palace of Versailles. The builder knew exactly what he desired and how to build it. Is this showing the future when future clients will be able to choose their designs and instead of other humans, get robots, drones and 3D printers to build it for them?

Source: author.

Figure 2.4 Developer markets the contemporary 'architect designed home', London. Such labels give a sense of exclusivity and prestige to the project. Emotional, rather than deliberative, responses can drive financial decisions

Source: author.

Practice of architecture   65

per 3,000 employees and also separate savings from an energy-efficient design (scoring good brownie points for a energy company). In another study, offices rated in the top 20 per cent for the quality of their design could charge rents 22 per cent higher than those rated in the bottom 20 per cent. Tangible evidence of benefit can be a powerful motivation for desire. However, such evaluation has limitations, as we have seen in the case of trying to quantify values. First, it has to be in the same sector to be convincing, i.e. you cannot show such figures for a residential project to convince clients to commission you for an office project. Second, evaluation is usually a sound practice for larger projects, especially those that are publicly funded, of typologies that may be built again and again (such as schools and hospitals). Third, such figures have to be used in conjunction with other motivational factors, including desire, in order to attract more commissions. Fourth, one needs to invest time and money to harvest post-occupancy evaluation figures, an action that may be difficult to resource for a small practice. So, for the many small and new practices, increasing desire remains the best motivation for getting work and getting paid for it. Or luck.

In fact, luck may be the most important thing of all. One has to believe in luck because the alternative is a belief in meritocracy – 'well, you didn't work hard enough, so you didn't get the work'. According to the dictionary, luck is the force that causes things, especially good things, to happen to you by chance and not as a result of your own efforts or abilities. It has been said that luck is better than skill – there are many talented and clever people but not everyone is lucky. One of the most bizarre strokes of luck apparently aided the competition win of the Bastille Opera House.[25] The project was won by the then unknown 37-year-old Uruguayan architect Carlos Ott, based in Canada. The jury, it has been said, thought that the entry was from the more famous Richard Meier. Ott's luck in having someone on the jury who liked Meier's work was not something he could have planned for. Buoyed by that initial success, Ott has since gone on to more success with work in Canada, the Middle East and elsewhere. Looking at a historical example, we find Joseph Paxton, whose luck helped him (although doubtlessly he was a hard worker and talented too). His biggest stroke of luck was meeting the Duke of Devonshire, William Cavendish, who happened to be strolling in the garden when Paxton was working. Impressed by his enthusiasm, Cavendish appointed him as his head gardener, despite his tender age of 20 and being without much experience. At that post, he cultivated the Cavendish banana, now the most consumed banana in the Western world and developed greenhouse designs. Other connections (including

66 Practice of architecture

marriage) and work followed. Besides being a landscape architect, he also designed the Crystal Palace and his eclectic career included being Member of Parliament for the city of Coventry.

Free work vs. promotion

There is a big difference between free work and promotion – something that many architects, especially new ones, do not understand. Promotion is about advertising your service and creating desire for that service, while free work is about desperation. For instance, a newly established open source platform founded by an architect is making contemporary residential designs available by letting people download house blueprints for free, with the intention of stimulating debate between designers and clients. Their website tries to entice clients:

> Hiring a world-class architect is something not many people can afford. You want a bespoke house? You're gonna have to pony up a lot of money. [G]ood design has become a luxury; a snooty, out-of-reach idea that only the rich have access to, which is actually the exact opposite of what good design should be.[26]

They have signed up new and upcoming architects. I cannot imagine any other profession offering services for free, and I cannot see how this would make architecture more accessible to the public nor how any architect could make money from this. Also 'free work' is not covered by personal indemnity insurance. I have also tried the 'barter economy' by offering architectural work in return for other services, but that has not been successful and, of course, it will be impossible to justify that to my insurers if something did go wrong. New practices can also be seen to be trying to do too much – a young architect, in her enthusiasm, not only provides a downloadable booklet about 'how to avoid costly mistakes in planning a conversion' but also has promised 'free advice booklets on energy efficient self-build, eco-extensions, saving you money on your energy bills, eco upgrades to listed buildings and more … information'.[27] Apart from mortgage brokers (and busy bodies), I know of no other service providers who give out such free advice. And mortgage brokers get their commissions and fees one way or the other. So what can we learn from other service providers?

Consider Gmail, which has two versions – free and a paid-up version – and costs $5 per month. The paid version has features such as customised email addresses, guaranteed 24/7 operations and support, twice the storage capacity, no adverts and a connection to Google Apps Marketplace. Both services come with no additional work from Google, i.e. everything is set up – all you do is choose one of the services. Similarly, architects need to spell out what they can do for 'free' and what benefits the client will receive if the work is paid for, which could include planning assessments, insurance cover, etc. Architectural service is a bespoke service (as opposed to Google), so it is even more important that we study the brief and say what we can do, and propose reasonable fees. The Crown Commercial Service in the UK, which procures services from SMEs for government contracts, advises them to have a three-pronged approach when bidding for work: offering the service with a lower price through efficiency savings; offering a different service for the same price; and offering 'enhanced' services for higher fees. If you can offer all these alternatives and thereby create some flexibility, the buyer will like this because a single supplier can provide them with choices.

PR for architects, or why your clients don't understand you

Architects need to be able to promote themselves effectively and ambitiously. This seems to have been no problem in the old days. Imhotep, an Egyptian architect who lived in 2600 BCE, had an official title that would have been impressive enough for anyone: 'Chancellor of the King of Egypt, Doctor, First in line after the King of Upper Egypt, Administrator of the Great Palace, Hereditary Nobleman, High Priest of Heliopolis, Builder, Chief Carpenter, Chief Sculptor and Maker of Vases in Chief.' However, to do this now in the twenty-first century, especially in the UK where modesty and self-deprecation are essential values, would be quite difficult. There appears to be no one to blow the trumpet on our behalf either – remember, RIBA promotes architecture, not architects. But Sir Norman Foster says that 'advocacy is the only power an architect ever has'.[28]

First, there is the public's difficulty in understanding what architects do. For example, some 450 years after the word 'architect' was coined, 15 per cent of Britain's population do not know what an architect does. As part of the survey, which was also carried out by YouGov in 2012,[29] 2,031 British adults were asked to select things that they thought an architect does from a list of tasks, all of which incidentally can be done by architects:

68   Practice of architecture

- 15 per cent did not know that architects design buildings.
- 22 per cent did not know that they prepare detailed construction drawings for building projects.
- 48 per cent did not know that architects prepare specifications to be used for building projects.
- 69 per cent did not realise architects negotiate planning permission with the local authorities (while 72 per cent did not know they apply for planning permission in the first place).
- 86 per cent were not aware that architects select, negotiate with and manage all the contractors.
- And a massive 91 per cent did not know that they run the financial accounts for building projects.

The second problem with our interaction with the public is that our idea of aesthetics is at variance with them. Countless times we read about 'terrible, ugly buildings' that people complain about and then are amazed when they are told that this is an award-winning building. In a poll in the August 2015 issue of British Airways' *High Life* magazine, for example, the Shard was the most popular building for people, but the final panel composed of architects and historians voted it out. The newly refurbished Birmingham station costing £750 million, adorned with a curved roof that brings daylight into the foyer and a new concourse, has had mixed reactions. According to the BBC, some passengers said it was 'stunning and imaginative, with beautiful lines'.[30] However, one said that platforms and trains would still be overcrowded as 'aesthetics don't improve function', and another passenger told BBC Midlands Today that she felt the station was 'hideous', with 'style over substance *as usual with modern design*' (my emphasis).[31] This is a universal problem. Steven Bingler, an architect from the USA, recounts his 88-year-old mother's reaction to a model showing a pair of stacked boxes, sheathed in corrugated metal, built by architecture students from the University of Virginia: 'It looks like somebody piled a couple of boxcars on top of each other, then covered them up with cheap metal and whatever else they could find at the junkyard!'[32] Bingler says that it could be easy to dismiss his mother as an unsophisticated layperson. Instead, he says that we should be producing work that the public can understand and relate to.

There is a resistance to the idea amongst architects that people should always 'understand' design. I ask: why shouldn't people understand the design, especially if you want them to pay for it?

Practice of architecture 69

For a piece of art, it hardly matters if anyone understands it or not, likes it or not and buys it or not. No one is forced to look at or use a piece of art, but a building is a different matter. Architecture does not come with the freedom of choice of use that a piece of art does. But now even artists are demanding that taxpayer cash be spent on art only the public understand and that public funding be only given to work that is 'both popular and profound'.[33] Both history and research on design tells us that people need time to get used to new things. It is not just that the public does not appreciate well-designed things. They just are afraid of investing money into something that could be a life-time purchase, as a house is, and things going wrong. They do not realise that the cost of design is a fraction of the total construction cost, is insignificant in comparison to the maintenance and operating costs of the building over its lifetime, and it is worth investing in the skills of design professionals as early as possible in the process when they can add the most value.

However, this fear of architecture could be something more complex and more than personal, as the playwright David Greig describes:

> I think that the public suspicion of architecture is more than just a fear of the new. The institution of architecture, those who build and those who commission buildings, are seen, I believe correctly, as a powerful establishment elite. Worse, they are seen as a metropolitan, pretentious, moneyed elite. Precisely the type of elite that the British most dislike.[34]

This is the complex fear built over a century that RIBA must tackle, and not just by having exhibitions about Brutalism or other architectural concepts. The architect and the architecture student can also help to alleviate this fear by engaging with the local community in which they live and by working on socially relevant projects. For this we need to engage with the ordinary person, not just big clients. Both the Farrell review and RIBA's own report 'Client and architect: Developing the essential relationship' entirely missed any input from small domestic clients, who provide the biggest source of work for architects.

Engagement with people does not mean a dumbing down of design or not proposing new ideas – take, for example, the Byker Wall project mentioned in Chapter 1. The advice from the successful businessman to our discussion group was that we should remember that business is non-judgemental. He asked us to listen to the voice of the ordinary person, read stuff that you normally wouldn't and do things that you have not done before. And clients have insights into designs that our creative or habitual efforts might turn a blind eye to. For instance, in 2007, 13 architectural firms were invited to create designs for a neighbourhood in New Orleans, USA, devastated by Hurricane Katrina. Architects had based their designs on the iterations of the modernist family home, but the community was not impressed: 'What's with the flat roofs? You know it rains here, a lot, right?'[35]

Architecture also has to compete for public attention with other arts such as film, theatre, literature, art and music, which are much more direct and accessible. Although the Stirling Prize and the Carbuncle Cup are bringing some knowledge of good and bad architecture to the public, it is time that architects also took responsibility for that lack of discernment. After all, if people cannot distinguish between good and bad design and do not worry about the quality of where they live and work, then it affects us all. The managing director of a PR company wrote in 2011: 'Many architects rarely get the credit they deserve for their work. And I don't just refer to headline public realm projects. I refer to jobs such as social housing schemes, schools, commercial buildings.'[36] It would appear that engaging with the public, such as holding exhibitions about your work away from institutional or arty venues, would enable people to engage with you and your work – they would be able to see the 'ordinary good' that architects do. The director of another PR consultancy put it simply and directly: 'PR is about relations with the public. It is not, as assumed, relations with the press only.'[37] She also advises architects to find champions and supporters in order to get work and to network. She also thinks that if architects can find ways of being visible publicly in a positive way, not only will it bring work but also bring the architectural debate out to the public realm.

Most architects think that PR is an unnecessary expense – RIBA's 2013–2014 Benchmarking report recommended that up to 5 per cent of practice turnover should be spent on marketing and up to 10 per cent to break into a new sector. Most small practices in the UK do not have in-house PR, only large ones do. At one of the creative soirées, there was a very successful businessman whose wife is an architect with a well-known big practice. His advice to architects was to get an agent in the way that 'all creative people need agents'. But if you cannot afford one, become your own agent. Salvador Dali painted, acted, designed, wrote and danced until he became a one-man PR agent for

Practice of architecture   71

himself. His provocations were seen as gimmicks by his critics and as 'performance art' by his fans. Not all of Dali's creative ventures succeeded, but what succeeded was enough to give him a place in history. But architects think this might be too vulgar because they think that their work itself is self-promotion. A PR director mentioned the case of an architect who said: 'I don't need PR. My work sells itself. If I design a great building, it is there forever, a permanent advert.'[38] But have they seen anyone entering a building and asking about its architect? The November 1993 edition of *RIBAJ* carried an article about how most people surveyed did not know what architects did and did not know their names, including the most famous of that day, Norman Foster and Richard Rogers. More than 20 years later, when I mention these names, not many people know them or the buildings they designed, even though they might have used them.

Real PR is not a whitewash to cover bad news. It should not be a spin. A medium-sized practice I spoke to said that if they have bad news, they prefer not to say anything to the press because 'it goes away on its own'. However, silence may not be the golden option for all situations – some stories run forever, and sometimes notoriety may be good too. Some stories need specialist advice before publication, while other stories need unified statements from different interested or affected parties. Amanda Baillieu writes about the 'brands' that architects of the past such as Soane and Adams created, without, of course, using the word 'brand' through their illustrated monographs.

> Just like those eighteenth-century architects, successful practices today commission the best photographers, writers and model makers to lend their work a sheen and credibility to appeal to prospective clients. But in their bid for fame and fortune they edit out the difficult bits. This is partly because they believe that keeping their business model, technology and processes under wraps gives them a competitive advantage. It's also because architecture is not interested in why projects fail. 'We can't say what really happened because if we did we'd never work again' is the common refrain.[39]

According to a PR director, good PR is honest and transparent. She says that while there are not many crises in architecture that are of public interest, there are always good stories that the architect can promote. This can be done via social media and both trade and general press. Another PR director says that there are opportunities at every

72   Practice of architecture

stage of building for stories to keep people informed and interested and advises media coverage at various stages of development: planning approval, start on site, site nears completion, site launch, etc.

One of the best ways to promote good design is to have good images of the buildings and people on your website. John Soane recorded his work meticulously, not just for posterity but also to get new work and ideas. Soane made almost 8,400 drawings of his own designs (many drawn by his assistants), with over 600 covering his biggest commission, the Bank of England. He used these for his lectures at the Royal Academy. Just imagine doing such a large numbers of drawings without computers, using only ink and paper. The lesson is that drawings always become a point of debate and discussion. A new building, or even a proposal for a new building, attracts media attention (remember the outrageous images of Archigram?). But choose your images carefully. Not all buildings are photogenic, let alone newsworthy. And it is not good PR to have only fictional architecture on your website – people want to see built work too. Catchy practice names are good; many new practices have a touch of building about them – Make, Erect, Weave, Assemble, Stitch, Stand, etc.[40]

What is your unique selling point? Think about your niche market, one PR director advised. A website that shows a diverse workplace full of people with happy and smiling faces appears to be a good place to work and to be associated with. Similar to photos of grumpy male architects, I am always worried about interiors of buildings with no people or plants – these show a lack of reality and empathy. Think about what possible clients might want to see. Okay, you might not want to have the photo and biography of the 'office dog', as one practice website does very bravely and humorously, but some show of humanity and untidiness might be good – after all, that is how most of us live.

Expressing and explaining ourselves

Our penchant to show empty monastic spaces has left us likened to practising a cult:

> Architecture, the most public of endeavours, is practised by people who inhabit a smugly hermetic milieu which is cultish. If this sounds far-fetched just consider the way initiates of this cult describe outsiders as the lay public, lay writers and so on: it's the language of the priesthood.[41]

In response, a commentator responded online:

Figure 2.5 As small business owners do not have the same resources to market their service or product as big businesses, they may have to be extra clever in winning over the competition as this kebab shop owner does. So whether you market yourself as the 'best' or 'best super' depends upon your ambitions and what you can realistically deliver

Source: author.

74 Practice of architecture

There are plenty of modest, empathetic architects – and architectural literature, for that matter – engaging with place, revelling in imperfection, taking inspiration from left-over spaces, interacting intensively with their clients, improving our public spaces and our built environment in general.[42]

However, as we know, these kind of architects who do common good, do not attract media attention. Research shows that architects are happy, creative and compassionate people.[43] These qualities sustain us in our work as well as our personal lives. Other adjectives about architects – arrogant, bullying, aloof, etc. – contrast with sexy (apparently we are the sexiest professionals, but only the male architects!), eloquent, creative, etc. Antonio Gaudi, the twentieth-century architect, is even on the way to becoming a saint. We appear to be a profession of extreme personalities to the public. Why is this so? Steven Bingler seems to know:

The world would be a drearier place without Fallingwater, the Guggenheim Bilbao and the Sydney Opera House. The problem isn't the infinitesimal speck of buildings created by celebrity architects (some arresting, some almost comic in their dysfunction), but rather the distorting influence these projects have had on the values and ambitions of the profession's middle ranks. We've taught generations of architects to speak out as artists, but we haven't taught them how to listen.[44]

But the real problem is that we do not know that we are not listening. So, research and surveys continue to indicate people do not know what architects do and we continue to be bewildered by the hostility to the profession. The Carbuncle Cup[45] for the ugliest buildings, started by *Building Design* in 2006, is more eagerly awaited than the Stirling Prize which is given to the best building. And why shouldn't it be so – 'A doctor can bury their mistakes, the architect can't', and so architecture remains a potent physical presence of good or bad – for anyone can throw eggs at it, or as Bingler explains: 'In architecture, everyone is a critic.'[46]

David Greig, the playwright, says:

My play 'The Architect' was inspired by a story I heard in a pub. It goes something like this: the man who designed a particular Glasgow housing estate was so traumatised when he saw the ugliness of his finished work that he climbed to the highest tower on the estate and jumped off. A month or so later, in a different pub, I heard the same story told about an estate in Hackney, then again about an estate in Newcastle. I heard the story told over and over again about different places but always about the ultimate death by suicide of an architect. However, as far as I can discover from my research no architect has ever jumped to his death from his own building. The suicidal architect is an urban myth. It struck me, however, that the myth perhaps gives voice to a collective psychic wish for revenge upon the creators of our urban environment. Perhaps the British public yearn to see architects fall to their deaths from the top of high buildings. Subconsciously, of course.[47]

The problem about understanding architecture is seen primarily as art, not technology or place-making. David Greig continues: 'Architects have "visions", their buildings contain "metaphor", "reference" and "analogy". Building styles are "isms". Discussions about architecture take place within the same world and with the same vocabulary as discussions about art.'[48] While the public are being encouraged to be creative in a nationwide campaign by the BBC backed by various celebrities in 2015,[49] notwithstanding that (or perhaps because of that) everyone is ready to take a pot shot at architects and architecture and debate about its relevance. Just imagine if everyone did that to other professions such as doctors or lawyers. It is easy to have divisive opinions about modern or abstract art, and so naturally architecture is also a prime target. But architecture is not just art to be commented, admired or loathed from afar – it is inhabited and used. It serves a practical purpose and therefore needs to be considered in context to its rightful place in society.

So if architecture is not understood, then how are we to make it less misunderstood and more accessible? Would it not be to our advantage to make ourselves understood? But instead we talk to the converted only or to other architects – our work is shown in architectural institutions such as RIBA or in exclusive art exhibitions such as the Venice Biennale, or featured in exclusive art house magazines where architecture is tagged along with travel, interiors, fashion, etc. Resistance or oblivion to architectural debate might stem from our schooling where we learn nothing much about our built environment. People who come to demonstrate against various building proposals in the local council's planning department come because they have not been included in the design process or their views are not taken into account, leading to misunderstanding of the final work or even disagreement.

76 Practice of architecture

But we neither listen nor explain. With our bodies cloaked in various shades of black, our language also alludes to the mystical and magical (and sometimes comical) – therefore also exclusivity, with occasional comical results. At one of the pavilions in the 2015 Venice Biennale, I asked the guide: 'What has the architect done here?' To which she solemnly gave me a pamphlet, which read:

> The structure shifts between historicity and modernism. [The architect] removes the building's historicizing architectural elements from sight by means of a black monolith that seems to hover under the ceiling casting its shade on the entire floor space of the pavilion, and a black floor construction that eliminates the pavilion's different levels. At the same time, [his] complex intervention relativizes the bounds between architectural space and nature, inside and outside ... How can one adequately contribute to an environment based on nation-state representativity where individual voices constantly compete for maximum attention? What phenomena are meaningful in such a context?'

So I asked her: 'Does this mean that the ceiling and floor have been painted black so that the columns appear to float?' 'Yes,' she replied. We love complexity, using big and confusing words, like when an architect describes himself as a 'researcher whose interest lies at the nexus of innovative means of participation through design and heterotopian architecture in violent spaces'.[50] At a healthcare design conference I attended, the architect described herself as working in 'preventative urbanism'.[51] An award-winning student project was titled 'Heteroglossic city: A polemic against the managerial urban paradigm of critical reconstruction in Berlin'. New technology has spawned forth even more jargon. If we can speak to each other in such mumbo jumbo, it is no wonder that the general public cannot understand us.

The proper language for debate about the shape of our cities and buildings must be in the language of the everyday, amongst ordinary people. 'Architecture should be the stuff of tabloid comment not arts page gossip,' says Greig.[52] I agree, but uninformed discourse may be equally destructive. So how about a respected architectural columnist writing for *The Sun*, the most-read newspaper in the UK?[53] Outrageous though the idea sounds, this won't be a first. For 40 years, Osbert Lancaster, the architectural historian, created satirical cartoons for the *Daily Express*, making descriptions such as 'Stockbroker Tudor' and 'Wimbledon Transitional' part of the common vocabulary. He knew that humour would break down social barriers. The Fuck parades against the gentrification of London (and the demonstration in front of the RIBA building before the 2015 Gold Medal presentations) are a sign of the profound disagreement between the profession's vision and the public's needs. However, such clashes still raise an awareness of the problems and continue the discourse, more than a practice winning the top art prize will ever do. An architect explained: 'What we do enriches lives and makes people happier, wealthier and healthier. Unless we can convince [them] at this basic, utilitarian level we are not going to get the recognition our art form deserves.'[54]

Ethical practice

In 2014, I had joined the RIBA Ethics Group to examine the complex nature of design and building work and how naivety and ignorance are not excuses for working unethically. Common with other professions, architects have a duty of care towards their clients and the wider society – it is part of the code of conduct. It may be easy to self-regulate by taking care of small things (such as keeping clients informed, getting statutory consents or taking notes); however, continued minor misdemeanours and shoddy practice can be harmful to any practice. Other industries such as clothing and fashion are transforming themselves into models of corporate social responsibility, albeit after major disasters such as the Rana Plaza in Bangladesh, so why not in architectural practice? Risk assessments may often tease out these problems before they become a danger but, in small projects or projects done in countries with less technical knowledge or enforcement of codes, there is the possibility that molehills may become mountains too soon. However, one does not have to be working abroad to be accused of working unethically – according to Action for Social Housing, the elitism of new housing is unethical because it propagates inequality. They accused RIBA of 'violating' paragraph 5 of the ARB's code of conduct (to consider the wider impact of your work) and argued that architectural award ceremonies such as the Stirling Prize give 'cultural legitimacy to the class war being waged through housing in Britain today'.[55]

In the UK, where the majority of practices are small practices of less than ten people, one cannot be too complacent – small practice does not mean sloppy practice. Time and money constraints are two things that appear to be responsible for a disregard of ethics. Ethical considerations are sacrificed on the altar of large construction projects that need to be finished on time and on budget. So not surprisingly this

Figure 2.6 Protestors in front of the Chinese embassy which stands opposite RIBA. In November 2010, Ai Wei Wei, the dissident Chinese artist, warned architects working in China that they were complicit in its human rights abuses. Treading carefully between ethics and business can be a difficult process for architectural practices

Source: author.

often results in deaths and injuries plus the large-scale destruction of natural and man-made environments. Architecture is dependent upon patronage – it follows the money. When projects have to be finished on time and on budget, who wants to worry about where the materials came from as long as the client is happy? Politicians are also happy to oblige. But as a newspaper reader complained: 'The FIFA scandal did not kill anybody but the building of stadiums did, so why are not more people talking about it?'[56]

British architects are working all over the world, particularly the 'BRIC' nations – Brazil, Russia, India and China – as well as other emerging economies in Africa and Asia. Overseas offices of British practices are extremely cosmopolitan, especially in places such as New York.[57] Even smaller practices are working globally, taking advantage of the time differences to complete projects in record time. While the RIBA Building Futures survey predicts that global interdisciplinary consultancies will have one of the greatest opportunities for future growth,[58] working overseas is beset with problems. For one, it means working on sites with poor health and safety conditions, amidst indifferent planning systems, chronic shortages, institutional weaknesses, resulting in delays. The procurement and administrative systems and statutory regulations currently in use in non-Western countries have been inherited from a colonial past from countries with markedly different histories, cultures and construction expertise, so archaic and self-defeating practices remain embedded in the process.[59] In 2001, the International Labour Organization conducted research that highlighted the poor condition of construction sites in poor countries.[60] But things are not really changing – the loss of life and buildings including historic sites in the 2015 earthquake in Nepal could have been much less had design and construction practices been more sound, echoed in the phrase 'Earthquakes don't kill people, buildings do'.

The second paradoxical issue is that these construction problems are often solved by 'shortcuts' such as bribery, the use of slave labour or sourcing materials in a way that is damaging to the environment, etc., as the ethical delivery of buildings can get in the way of 'good business'.[61] Poor ethical standards may not be intentional, but equally ignorance cannot be an excuse. As Jeremy Till says, 'No architect sets out to behave badly or to inflict unhappiness in the world; the problem is that their priorities as to what constitutes the good are so misplaced'.[62] Using architects to build colonies on illegally appropriated land, removing or destroying architectural artefacts are other ways that architecture may become a tool of repression and power – but this method is not new to the modern world. So how do we differentiate between what is 'good enough' vs. competent, or best practice vs. professionalism while building overseas?

80 Practice of architecture

The ethical and moral dilemmas of modern practice are very complex, so each practice has to decide for itself what it can or cannot do. It need not be a long list of things that may become self-defeating. But they have to be challenging enough for the practice. For instance, Bauman Lyons Architects has made a simple mission statement that encompasses their ethical and environmental stance:

> An important principle in sustainable development lies in harnessing best practice from international and national experience and combining it with the understanding of the local. The first is possible through mobility and technology but the latter can only be secured through staying in a place and contributing to making it worth staying in. These are the principles that guide our practice.[63]

In other words, this small practice has chosen to work within a small catchment area – a commitment that is difficult yet doable. Each practice can set its own ethical standards. By elevating the basic professional standard through setting their work in social and environmental contexts, each practice will be able ensure that they survive locally and globally. So while autotelic architects may have to compete with practices of emerging economies that may have lower overheads and work at a faster rate, they can raise the bar for all by aspiring to higher ethical standards. This will set off a chain for positive improvements in global construction.

In 2015, on the recommendation of the RIBA Council, the institute became a signatory to the United Nations Global Compact (UNGC). The UNGC is a set of ten high-level principles promoting best practice in areas covering human rights, labour rights, the environment and anti-corruption. RIBA has committed to support and promote these principles internally and externally by encouraging these values through RIBA practices. In particular, RIBA has committed to the following:

1   Provide a forum for the debate of the universal principles enshrined in the UNGC as they apply to the practice of architecture, in particular in relation to health, safety and welfare, diversity and inclusion, and environmental sustainability.
2   Encourage and support RIBA Chartered Practices in addressing the universal principles of the UNGC as a strategic issue at board/ management level.
3   Facilitate access to tools and guidance that can assist architects in responding to ethical issues that are beyond the scope of legal and/or code of conduct definitions.

Practice of architecture 81

4 Encourage chartered practices to use their influence to promote the principles of the UNGC throughout their construction project supply chains.
5 Collaborate with other professional organisations to review professional codes of conduct.
6 Commit to continuously improve the social and environmental impacts of RIBA.

Again, although RIBA has adopted this, like its own equal opportunities policy, there is no compulsion on any practice to adopt it. But given the outcry against bad work practices abroad, it would be useful for the bigger practices or those working overseas to adopt it. The MacEwen Award launched by *RIBAJ* in 2015 demonstrates that ethics and social good in architecture are essential as 'Architecture for the Common Good'.[64] The award aims to 'celebrate the best examples in the UK and Ireland of projects with a clear social benefit, right across society [that] recognise that an ethical approach is a key part of good design'.

The most valuable are people

Over twenty-five years ago, Peter Buchanan wrote about design values:

> To design is the prime motive for being an architect; skill at it is the prime determinant of status in the profession. An architect might be a bad builder, a bungling businessman, a tyrant with colleagues, consultants and contractors; and yet if a designer [is] of exceptional talent all this is forgiven – even to the squandering of the client's money on something of little value beyond being a manifesto of that talent.[65]

It is difficult to imagine this kind of person being an exceptional architect or a success now. Everything from ethical principles, good employment practice, procurement, business sustainability, etc. is part of modern architectural practice – the kind of mad genius described by Buchanan that will be out of work pretty soon today and may be hauled before the ARB or an employment tribunal.

Architects, whether in large offices or small ones, work closely in teams. So hiring people who can fill the gaps makes for the best team according to employers. Once a good team has been chosen, it is important to invest in them. Junior staff members would benefit from

82   Practice of architecture

mentoring and training, and so would 'returners' (people who take time off for maternity or paternity leave, long sickness, sabbaticals, etc.). Students working in their year out also benefit from mentoring and training – but often practices see them as temporary staff. Students working in a practice often bring with them innovative ideas from academic work that might be beneficial to the practice. Staff retention may be difficult for small practices because of the shifting work load and because digitisation offers the freedom to 'moonlight' or move to other lucrative work. However, retaining staff as long as possible is a more prudent choice because training new staff can work out to be expensive (about £20,000) and time consuming.

Small and lesser-known practices can take comfort from the news that the biggest or the most admired architectural firms in the world are not necessarily the best people to work for. In 2015, the top three firms among all construction professionals to work for were all architectural practices. Eighteen other architectural practices made up the list of 50 construction firms, or more than one-third of the list.[66] Using surveys and interviews, the winner, who is an 'Investors in People' firm, was praised as a 'truly outstanding employer'. Its maternity and paternity packages and staff loyalty scheme, which involves air tickets and holidays, were mentioned by the judges. Taxis were provided for late workers (although it is not good practice to work late). A previous winner was described as consistently 'among the sector's most enlightened employers', with staff benefits packages, commitment to diversity and a new staff forum. Another small firm had flexible working and even a staff vegetable garden – whose produce was cooked in a kiln built by the office for company lunches. Good employment can reap lateral benefits. A practice based in Cornwall, whose staff regularly go out surfing and sailing, say that their awareness of coastal environments has enabled them to have designed schemes for other seaside locations such as Blackpool and Bournemouth. That small architecture firms, despite external problems, are committing to staff welfare is a reason for cheer.

But how does a small practice ensure a supply of work in order to retain staff and have good practices? One suggestion is to 'keep looking for work, even when you have work'.[67] Keep developing new projects slowly while you work on current ones, which should be about one-half or two-thirds of your work. Less than one-third should be future projects, which may not be all speculative or competition work, as those can be very expensive for the small practice (though a small part of future work can be like that, but again do not depend on that). If work is prioritised, then it is possible to always have some work as current, some for the immediate future and some for the discernible future. According to Grant Thornton, the accounting and management consultants who have a unit dedicated to insolvencies and work with architects, spending time on 'value creation' is as important as day-to-day work in the medium term. Value creation includes innovation, making the right strategic choices and risk management. Networking is a free and useful source of work – remember Soane's example. The architect Sarah Wigglesworth once said that one must forget education or grades – the thing is to 'network like mad'.[68] It is important not to just network with other architects only but also to include co-professionals and non-professionals. By creating what are called 'weak links' and casual non-work-related contacts, the chances of getting work also increases. You are more likely to get a lucky break from those 'weak' contacts than from work-related contacts – all of whom are equally determined to win the work themselves. You can build a network of people you connect with occasionally. Keep tabs on them and feed them with useful information from time to time.

Currently creative arts, including architecture and design, add £71 billion to the economy (bringing £8 million per hour) and employ 1.7 million people.[69] The arts and culture sector accounts for 0.4 per cent of UK GDP or 1.1 per cent of total UK employment,[70] yet the work done by these creative people attracts more than £856 million of tourist spending. The latest ONS statistics show an interesting trend from Victorian times to now. Despite the low return, the service industries (which include arts, entertainment and recreation[71]) are on the rise, while commerce and manufacturing industries (construction, energy, water, agriculture and mining) are going down. In 1948, UK service industries contributed an estimated 46 per cent to UK GDP, and by 2012 this had increased to 78 per cent.[72]

To have a vibrant and creative society as well as a financially sustainable one, we need architects and designers. Almost every month, the ARB tells us that someone has been fined for misusing the title architect. So if people are ready to break the law for it, it tells us that 'architect' is still a coveted title. The 3,500 hits that RIBA's 'Find an architect' gets a day tells us that architects are needed. On a more mundane level, this got me thinking about what would happen if there were no architects. What if we were condemned to spend our lives in terrible buildings, use badly designed cutlery, drive unsafe cars or ... (put here the myriad ways in which an invisible army of designers have made our lives easier)? Good design is certainly invisible – it

84 Practice of architecture

is only when things go wrong that people complain. Designers spend a long time making things that give us delight and practical use. As Kenneth Clark has pointed out,

> one could tell more about a civilisation from its architecture than from anything else it leaves behind. Painting and literature is to some extent dependent largely on unpredictable individuals. But architecture is to some extent a communal art – at least it depends upon a relationship between the user and the maker more closer than in other arts.[73]

So it is good to remind ourselves that as we go about our day-to-day business of work, architects and architecture do matter.

Notes

1 Nearly £10,000 in today's money.
2 Pevsner (1997).
3 Although this quote has been attributed to Peter Drucker, it has been attributed to many others too, going as far back as the 1500s. www.matthewcornell.org/blog/2007/7/30/whats-your-feed-reading-speed.html#1 (accessed January 2016).
4 'Why do women leave architecture?', RIBA, 2003.
5 From an exhibit by Laurie Baker at an exhibition of his work at the Architectural Association, London, 1997.
6 www.linkedin.com/pulse/20141017163342-42736566-architects-and-their-time?trk=mp-reader-card (accessed March 2016).
7 'All of a piece', *RIBAJ*, November 2013, p. 62.
8 Newport (2016).
9 www.virgin.com/entrepreneur/opting-out-email-well-and-good (accessed April 2016).
10 www.bbc.co.uk/news/business-33541865 (accessed October 2015).
11 'Value added', *RIBAJ*, November 2013, p. 60.
12 www.linkedin.com/pulse/20141017163342-42736566-architects-and-their-time?trk=mp-reader-card (accessed March 2016).
13 Ibid.
14 www.bbc.co.uk/news/magazine-33613246 (accessed April 2016).
15 www.bdonline.co.uk/comment/opinion/we-did-all-that-research-andyou-did-what?!/5077021.article (accessed September 2015).
16 'Adapt and survive', *RIBAJ*, October 2015, p. 64.
17 RIBA, www.architecture.com/Files/RIBAProfessionalServices/Regions/NorthWest/Education/Part%203/StudyPacks2013/March2013LectureNotes/FeeCalculation,NegotiationandManagement-AdrianDobson.pdf (accessed November 2015).
18 Personal communication.
19 Ibid.

Practice of architecture   85

20 www.dqi.org.uk/case-studies (accessed April 2016).
21 Mavity and Bayley (2009, p. 149).
22 www.theguardian.com/commentisfree/2012/oct/26/new-build-homes-british (accessed June 2014).
23 Dolan *et al.* (2010, p. 8).
24 'The Turning Tide', *CAM 75*, p. 14.
25 Ayers (2003, p. 188).
26 http://paperhouses.co/about/what-we-do (accessed September 2014).
27 I have chosen to protect her identity.
28 www.theguardian.com/artanddesign/2015/nov/22/norman-foster-i-have-no-power-as-an-architect-sustainability?CMP=twt_gu (accessed November 2015).
29 https://yougov.co.uk/news/2012/09/03/archi-what (accessed November 2012).
30 www.bbc.co.uk/news/uk-england-birmingham-34312400 (accessed September 2015).
31 Ibid.
32 www.nytimes.com/2014/12/16/opinion/how-to-rebuild-architecture.html?smid=fb-share&_r=1 (accessed June 2015).
33 Julian Spalding, 'Purpose of arts', *Evening Standard*, 1 December 2014.
34 www.front-step.co.uk/wp-content/uploads/2011/05/Architecture-article-for-Scotsman.pdf (accessed November 2015).
35 www.nytimes.com/2014/12/16/opinion/how-to-rebuild-architecture.html?smid=fb-share&_r=1 (accessed June 2015).
36 www.freshfield.com/do-architects-need-pr-people (accessed October 2014).
37 Author interview, 29 January 2015.
38 www.freshfield.com/do-architects-need-pr-people (accessed October 2014).
39 www.bdonline.co.uk/comment/architecture-is-the-loser-if-we-censor-history/5073506.article (accessed January 2015).
40 My own practice, Ecologic, has had ongoing problems with a Chinese firm, who declared that they would be 'persistent' in trying to acquire my practice name.
41 Meades (2013).
42 'Architects are the last people who should shape our cities', *Guardian*, 18 September 2012.
43 www.archdaily.com/192349/are-architects-depressed-unhealthy-and-divorced (accessed March 2016).
44 www.nytimes.com/2014/12/16/opinion/how-to-rebuild-architecture.html?_r=0 (accessed May 2015).
45 The Turnip Cup is the art equivalent of the Carbuncle, to compete with the Turner Prize.
46 www.nytimes.com/2014/12/16/opinion/how-to-rebuild-architecture.html?_r=0 (accessed May 2015).
47 www.front-step.co.uk/wp-content/uploads/2011/05/Architecture-article-for-Scotsman.pdf (accessed November 2015).
48 Ibid.

86 Practice of architecture

49 www.bbc.co.uk/programmes/articles/3P7n390cZc3VBpn7cPn0F5T/about-get-creative (accessed November 2015).
50 www.thepolisblog.org/2011/12/retracing-koolhaas-singapore-songlines.html (accessed December 2015).
51 www.front-step.co.uk/wp-content/uploads/2011/05/Architecture-article-for-Scotsman.pdf (accessed November 2015).
52 The words 'urbanism' and 'hetero' are particularly popular at present for various additions and iterations. The previous year it was 'disruptive'.
53 Almost 14 million people read *The Sun* in print and online, compared to *The Guardian*, which has an architectural columnist but a readership of 5 million.
54 www.architectsjournal.co.uk/home/fraser-blames-fee-levels-and-tick-box-procurement-for-demise/8688190.fullarticle (accessed September 2015).
55 www.bdonline.co.uk/news/stirling-prize-ceremony-targeted-by-social-housing-activists/5077855.article (accessed October 2015).
56 www.bbc.co.uk/news/magazine-33019838 (accessed March 2016).
57 'One giant leap', *RIBAJ*, February 2014, p. 70.
58 RIBA Building Futures report, RIBA, London, 2011.
59 http://citeseerx.ist.psu.edu/viewdoc/download?doi=10.1.1.198.2916&rep=rep1&type=pdf (accessed November 2015).
60 www.ilo.org/public/english/standards/relm/gb/docs/gb283/pdf/tmcitr.pdf (accessed September 2015).
61 Nabeel Hamdi, speaking at an ethics seminar, 2 June 2015.
62 'Angels with dirty faces', *RIBAJ*, March 2009, p. 26.
63 http://baumanlyons.co.uk (accessed March 2016).
64 www.ribaj.com/culture/better-than-just-good-design (accessed September 2015).
65 'How architects design', *AJ*, 19 and 20 December 1990, p. 22.
66 www.bdonline.co.uk/5071704.article?origin=BDdaily (accessed November 2014).
67 Personal communication.
68 www.bdonline.co.uk/life-class-sarah-wigglesworth/5014664.article (accessed April 2011).
69 www.gov.uk/government/news/creative-industries-worth-8million-an-hour-to-uk-economy (accessed November 2015).
70 www.gov.uk/government/uploads/system/uploads/attachment_data/file/210060/bis-13-958-uk-construction-an-economic-analysis-of-sector.pdf (accessed July 2014).
71 According to the ONS, the service industries include: wholesale and retail trade; repair of motor vehicles and motorcycles; transportation and storage; accommodation and food service activities; information and communication; financial and insurance activities; real-estate activities; professional, scientific and technical activities; administrative and support service activities; public administration and defence; compulsory social security; education, human health and social work activities; and arts, entertainment and recreation.
72 www.ons.gov.uk/ons/rel/ios/index-of-services/february-2015/stb-ios-february-2015.html (accessed May 2015).
73 Clark (1999).

3 The autotelic education

As a 15-year-old bricklayer, John Soane worked in the offices of the architect George Dance to extend a grand country house, Pitzhanger Manor, in what is today Ealing. Later in his 40s, rich and famous (and knighted), Soane bought that house, demolishing everything except the bit that he and Dance had worked on and using his inspiration from Italy he rebuilt the existing house and its gardens. He already had a house in central London, which is now the Sir John Soane museum, with its collection of famous artworks, sculptures, furniture and artefacts, so this became his 'country residence' where he entertained guests. But the house had another purpose. He thought that his collection of architectural antiques might entice his two sons into studying architecture. Their mother was the daughter of a builder and also interested in architecture, accompanying Soane to many places to look at buildings. Despite being surrounded by a wealth of architecture, neither child was interested – one would go on to study law.[1] Soane also spent money on his grandson in the hope that he might study architecture, but neither did he. Soane's humble background did not prevent him from following his dream successfully, while his sons' daily encounters with architectural antiquities did not influence them into studying it further.[2] This shows that perhaps architectural studies are truly autotelic – an interest in architecture is not defined by genes or the environment, which is good news for those of us not living in grand houses.

So who is studying architecture today and why? Design and art are the fourth most popular courses at UK universities for both UK and foreign students. In 2014, architecture, building and planning courses saw an increase of 13 per cent. Of the ten 'best' schools of architecture in the world, four are in the UK – one of these is now deemed the 'best' place to study art and design. So men and women, domestic and foreign, flock to these institutions.[3] More than 44 per cent of architecture student membership is female. BAME students are also well represented

88 The autotelic education

on architecture courses, making up around 18 per cent of all architecture undergraduates (compared to 16 per cent of all undergraduates), and some communities, for example the Chinese community, are represented (at first degree level) above their representation in the population as a whole (a similar result was obtained for the 2004 CABE study into the diversity of architecture schools, for which I was a panel member).

Architecture schools[4] have also been accused of producing 'too many' architecture students – so many that there is not enough work for them. In the USA, where there are 55 schools of architecture more or less evenly spread among its 51 states and 320 million people, an architect put it this way: 'Where in the world are 5,100 graduates [to find] jobs in a profession with a 20–30 percent unemployment rate [in 2015]?'[5] Or take Italy with its 35 schools, with as many as an average of 3,000 students in one cohort where getting an appointment with a tutor takes many days of waiting. Many poor countries boast several architecture schools – RIBA validates many of these (35 schools of architecture based in countries ranging from Argentina, Peru and Bulgaria to even cash-strapped Greece). Costa Rica (with a population of nearly 5 million) has seven schools, based in the capital city of San Jose, and reportedly nearly 4,000 registered architects. India with its population of over 1.2 billion has 85 schools of architecture with some unusual names – Viva and Lovely (also apparently a 'Dark School of Architecture').[6] The UK has 49 schools of architecture.

Of course one may argue that just because someone has studied architecture, they do not need to practise it. The director of a new London school has declared that he would be 'unconcerned if students did not go on to complete the triad and become architects'.[7] Italy and many of the Scandinavian countries have many architecture students and yet not all of them practise it. That the Italians and Scandinavians have a great eye for design may be due to nurture, not just nature. Studying architecture makes for better future clients. Architecture is also a versatile area of study – it allows you to branch off into many diverse sectors in an autotelic manner. As long as it does not become a financial burden, having many people who have an appreciation for arts and architecture can only be a good thing for society.

RIBA's role in architectural education

RIBA is involved in architecture courses around the world – apart from the UK, it validates 35 architecture schools in 20 other countries, involving more than 20,000 students. In addition, RIBA

The autotelic education   89

manages the validation system on behalf of the International Union of Architects (UIA), which covers the education of architects in a further 45 countries including Japan and Russia, thus involving another 30,000 students.[8] The Liverpool School of Architecture was established in 1894 and became the first university in the UK to award a RIBA-accredited degree in architecture. But for nearly 100 years, things continued as before in many places – architecture students worked for other architects and, as they gained experience and confidence, they set up offices themselves and trained others. A Congress on Architectural Education was held in 1924, which decried the pupillage system, which 'still lingers in certain localities', and clearly placed the emphasis on full-time training in 'Recognised Schools'. RIBA's domination of the validation process started in 1931 when all architects had to sit examinations set by RIBA and undergo pupillage (work experience) with a chartered practice.

Validation by RIBA is not free for the schools. All new schools (whether within or outside the EU, the procedures do not differentiate) pay an initial £7,500 administrative charge for an exploratory board (the first formal visit to consider the programme of architecture for candidate course status). Schools must also pay all travel and subsistence costs for the board members and a RIBA staff member. There is no further administrative charge for any future full visits, but schools must meet all travel and subsistence costs for board members and RIBA staff members. In the event of a course or courses, or examination, being 'conditioned', the school is responsible for bearing all the costs of a revisit (i.e. travel, accommodation, subsistence and incidental expenses). There is also an additional administration charge of £500 payable to RIBA to contribute to RIBA staff costs connected with correspondence, logistical arrangements and documentation.[9] The 'full board' visit takes place over two days. Visiting boards to schools are usually held every five years. The schools prepare documents and lay out exhibitions of student work to demonstrate they have complied with RIBA requirements.[10] Staff and students are interviewed as part of the process.

The validation team, which includes architects, co-professionals, a lay member, academics and a student (or new graduate) representative, is led by one architect or academic and supported by a vice chair and a secretary. All academics, architects and student or graduate members of the validation panel must be RIBA members. These team members are not paid for their work but get their rewards in other ways, as this statement from a former board member shows:

90 The autotelic education

I found validation to be really stimulating and made me review my own architectural education. You get a fascinating glimpse of the inner workings of the various institutions and I found it quite easy to spot what makes it tick, what its differentiating factors are, etc. The amount and quality of information provided varied tremendously and tended to reflect the character of the school [and its leadership and management]. I found we always came to a satisfactory conclusion, sometimes with a lot of soul searching and compromise, but I always felt satisfied that our duty had been done fairly.[11]

Writing as far back as 1958 in a report on architectural education, Sir Leslie Martin said: 'The aims of training and the standards reached in these schools differ widely. So do the standards of entry and the quality of instruction.'[12] Despite efforts at standardisation that started after the publication of that report, the quality of architectural teaching is uneven around the world and, in some countries or schools, more or less emphasis may be placed on either design or technical proclivity. In the past, the architect, the builder and the engineer were the same people. The oldest surviving book on architecture, *De architectura* by Vitruvius, another polymath (soldier, engineer, author and designer), describes the design and construction of buildings, towns, clocks and machines as all being part of architectural studies. But today, the purpose and direction of architectural education in today's world remains a divisive and grey area.

The three-part system of education

The three-part format of studies was set in the 1960s.[13] In this format, students finish their undergraduate Part 1 in three years, work in an office for one year, come back to do their Part 2, work again for a year and then sit their Part 3 exams in order to register as architects. It is possible to do each part of the course at separate schools of architecture. The UK education system has kept the work experience part of the course, derived as it is from the pupillage system that it replaced. It should be simple but it works out to be more complicated. More than 50 years later, we are realising the burden of a course that is too long (on average it takes 9–10 years to get to registration) and too expensive for students. Further, the EU follows the 3+2 Bologna model,[14] with a three-year undergraduate degree, followed by a two-year, coursework-based Master of Architecture professional degree. But this system does not include the work experience as in the UK.

The autotelic education   91

Many other non-EU countries follow this model, including India and Australia.

One must question whose interest the three-part system of education serves. On a positive note, the three-part system keeps everything neat and allows the movement of students onto different courses, and to stop and start their education at different universities. But it also lengthens the time it takes to qualify and, in particular, affects women and those with caring responsibilities or low income. Research indicates that women[15] and those from BAME[16] backgrounds drop out of architecture – many after just three years of Part 1 – due to different reasons. However, as the statistics show, many male students also drop out of architecture before registration. There are also mature students, especially in the Diploma, who may take time out to work, gain experience and raise a family before commencing studies again. Reports suggest that concerns over rising fees were putting UK students off studying architecture due to the length of time it takes to qualify. There has been a criticism of the exclusive schools of architecture within the 'Russell Group' of universities for the elitism they foster, with one critic even making a connection with the Stirling Prize winners – over 80 per cent of past winners have come from such schools.[17]

Comparing it with medical studies, which are expensive and long as well, architecture does not stand out well:

- **There is no automatic guarantee of work after graduation.** After graduation, doctors work for the NHS to get full registration with the General Medical Council. The salaries may be low but work is guaranteed. Architecture is considered to be a 'boutique' profession, seen as a luxury, therefore it is difficult to get work.
- **The course of studies is expensive and long.** A British Medical Association survey for 2012–2013 showed that medical students' debt could be between £24,000 and £70,000.[18] According to surveys, architecture students incur debts of between £88,000 and £100,000 during the course of their studies.[19] With no guarantee of work after graduation, it takes longer to pay off student loans for architecture graduates. Further, due to the nature of the course, conventional loans and grants are difficult to get, while students on university courses recognised by the General Medical Council may be eligible for financial help from the NHS as part of their course.[20]
- **To become a specialist takes further investment of time and money.** During medical studies, it is possible to specialise within

92 The autotelic education

the course or during training while being paid, while in architecture this practice-based specialism comes after further study and many years of work. To become a conservation architect, for example, one may have to study a special course after graduation and then practise it for a while to get commissions.

- **Work involves long hours and low pay.** A graduate architect may find their work life similar to their academic life – they are again in a 'long hours, no money' culture. A senior architect, according to a RIBA Benchmarking study, may be paid around £45,000–50,000, while medical consultants may be earning upwards of £200,000, even though they may be working similar or even smaller numbers of hours.
- **The complexity of the present three-part course.** A course that dips into more than 25 fields including design, geography, social sciences, anthropology, IT, etc., interrupted by periods of practical work experience, makes for a challenging course (unlike planning or law, there is no 'transfer' course or a 'credit system', meaning one must study architecture all the way through to qualify for registration).

From 2013 to 2015,[21] RIBA undertook its most comprehensive review of architectural education in the UK for the past 50 years. The RIBA Council agreed to an option that integrates the broken pattern of study and work experiences in the current three-part system by offering a seven-year award that includes the possibility of work-based learning. This will come into force by September 2016 and bring the UK system in synergy with the EU. The other purposes of this move, I assume, is to make the course less expensive, more flexible to complete, quicker to get to registration and make students more employable – because the professional practice element of an architect's training – Part 3 – could begin much earlier in the second year of their studies.[22] Thus, it could even be possible for students, who pass every year, to join the ARB register seven years after beginning their undergraduate degree, like their EU counterparts. However, it does then make it more difficult for a student to change universities mid-course due to a change in circumstances or simply because they do not like it there. Also, it may well be that such an apologetic tweaking of the traditional system will not remove the main concerns of the profession and the new graduates. *The two main elements that are at the heart of the problem – low pay and lack of work for architects – cannot be solved by these changes to the course of studies.*

The autotelic education   93

Practising architects, especially the majority of those in small practices, say that the new proposal will affect them in many ways. Small practices fear that they might be deployed by stealth (and without compensation, support and training) to provide something the schools should provide. Even in the recent past, architects from small practices have set out their concerns about students not learning about the practicalities of architecture while at schools. They say that 'architecture is not a hobby; students cannot be expected to pick up such vital issues through "osmosis" while working on [office] projects'.[23] At present Part 2 and 3 students get a 'mentor' who supports them in their work experience, but practices fear that a formalisation of the process might mean more work for them than usual. With the new proposal, some fear that they might end up providing the design education as well.

Hurdles to work

It is difficult to offer an analysis of the proposed system starting in September 2016. But it may be obvious immediately that the hurdles to work will remain the same as before. Apart from the slight advantage of early graduation for those starting in the new 2016 regime, both types of graduates will have to show work experience in order to qualify under the UK validation system. RIBA remains insistent not just on the work experience but also that it should be carried out in the UK – which makes it rather impossible for all those unable to find work here. The 'Professional Experience and Development Record' (PEDR)[24] advises:

> You should work for at least 12 months in an EEA member state (including the UK), the Channel Islands or the Isle of Man. The remaining 12 months may be undertaken anywhere in the world. You should note that Part 3 is concerned with assessing applied knowledge and skill in relation to professional conduct and competence to practise as an architect *in the UK*. Therefore, RIBA strongly recommends that at least 12 months of your experience is undertaken *in the UK*.
>
> (Emphasis added)

While it would be unlawful for the UK to prevent any EU-qualified architect who is registered in another EU member state from joining the ARB register, the hidden reality is that these new graduates

94 The autotelic education

from the EU may not be able to meet the requirements for RIBA chartered membership. Most countries of the EU produce far more architects than the UK, many of whom come to the UK to find work. The numbers of EU entrants to the UK register is rising – in 2013, the number of UK graduates was down by 9 per cent, while those from the EU rose by 8 per cent compared to 2012 – and this trend is continuing in 2014–2015. But do these nomadic graduates find work in the UK (or the EU)? In 2014, for example, nearly 200 architects from Spain, which is suffering from an economic crisis,[25] joined the UK register under mutual recognition arrangements. Most did not have any work experience because this experience is not required in Spain, but this is essential in the UK. Records show that only 4 per cent of Spanish graduates managed to find employment outside Spain in 2014. EU architects have cited relocation costs as well as language barriers as two of the problems associated with working in the UK. Thus, while the UK may have access to some of the EU's brightest and best students, in reality UK practices may not be able to take advantage of this. In contrast, medical and nursing graduates from the EU and beyond are able to find work in the UK – because work is available – and housing and training are provided by the NHS.

For overseas (non-EU) graduates, there are further problems. As the ARB does not recognise RIBA's validation of international schools, non-EU students have an even more tortuous and expensive route to registration. The prescribed examination fee is £1,671 per part of the ARB examination – therefore the total for Parts 1 and 2 would be £3,342. Add in the ARB registration fees, chartered membership and insurance, then you are looking at a figure of around £4,500 minimum.[26] That the ARB has no involvement in RIBA's international validation service appears to be a strange anomaly, and the assessment fees are astronomical. RIBA (together with the ARB) needs to iron out these problems, otherwise RIBA validations will be worthless to an overseas institution. (Then there are visa problems for new overseas graduates. The allocation of restricted Tier 2 visas, which allow entry of skilled migrant workers to the UK, will particularly affect small regional architectural offices, which will have to compete with London offices for international graduates.)

The starting salaries of graduates may be lower than an office secretary's, and there is evidence of bad practice – zero hour contracts, unpaid or poorly paid interns.[27] ZAP Architecture, who highlighted the effect of trebling university fees and the low starting salaries through an exhibition in 2011 at RIBA, said that students need to realise 'the knock-on effect this has on their own worth, as well as that of their future-architect-selves', while Architecture Students Network said that expecting graduates to 'work for free to gain PEDR experience will lead to further elitism with only those with the financial means able to take employment'.[28] Taking an unpaid internship has further financial repercussions for London students – it means no pay, while living costs (without transport) could add up to £5,500 for six months.[29] Incidentally, the 'living wage' policy may have unintended consequences due to people living and working for longer. The Department for Business, Innovation and Skills' official impact assessment of the policy says that higher pay for older workers could 'reduce the likelihood of employees leaving their jobs',[30] undermining opportunities for younger people under 25. This is particularly significant to architects because the average retirement age for an architect is five years more than the average pensionable age, and about 20 per cent of architects say that they would never retire.

Why is it so expensive to study architecture?

Architecture students incur unique expenses during their studies. First, architecture students have many additional expenses – expensive books, software, computer, printing and materials, and essential travel as part of their studies (and these can vary from school to school). Second, due to the length of the course, students are forced into borrowing more money to finish it off.[31] Third, the last part of the studies, Part 3, has to be self-funded, as only Part 1 and 2 students can take advantage of government loans. To fund their studies, UK students have a main finance package, which consists of essentially two parts – a Tuition Fee Loan and a Maintenance Loan (this is for full-time students only). London students receive a higher maintenance grant than others. Any additional academic expenses (which are often funded by parents or through savings) add to the burden of loan repayment. Interest on the accumulated debt is payable at a rate equal to the retail price index (RPI) measure of inflation, rising to RPI+3 per cent for higher earners. As of 2015, once earning an income of £21,000, the loan is repaid by taking 9 per cent of the monthly income using the PAYE system.[32]

96 The autotelic education

RIBA Part 2 Bursaries is a new funding scheme supporting architecture students looking to embark on a RIBA-validated Part 2 course within the UK. However, this is means tested,[33] and funding is for one year only. Some architectural practices may help by paying for the Part 2 course fees of a student who has worked in the practice or is working there. But this may restrict a student's portfolio and experience as they become tied to one practice. For some students, a UK maintenance grant is not even enough to pay the rent in most cities, especially London. Overseas students and student immigrants also struggle to get student loans. In September 2015, it was announced that there would be an interim policy that would allow qualifying applicants who had spent half their life in Britain and had at least three years of immigration status to get loans. In short, no matter one's status, it means that almost every architecture student in the UK will have to take out loans for their studies.

It has been calculated that to repay their debts, owing to inflation, an architecture student has to first find a high-paying job and stay in it for at least 30 years. Those who believe that incurring debts for studying is morally wrong are carrying out debt campaigns all over the world. Rolling Jubilee, an offshoot of the 'Occupy Wall Street' movement based in the USA, purchased and abolished $3.8 million (£2.35 million) of debt owed by 2,700 students. All German universities became free from September 2014 after fees were abandoned in Lower Saxony, the last of seven states to charge.[34] Campaigners in Hamburg claimed that tuition fees were socially unjust, and the state scrapped the charges in 2012. They said about the charges: 'They particularly discourage young people who do not have a traditional academic family background from taking up studies.'[35]

So while loan repayment affects all students, for an architecture student who has possibly the bigger debts, this is a particularly difficult situation. What can they do? If they study part time, it only serves to lengthen the course and does not entitle students to the maintenance part of the UK government loan. Some full-time students work night shifts or do other part-time work to get extra money. The pressure of loan repayment affects particularly low-income and disabled students and those with caring responsibilities. No wonder the number of UK students seeking places on domestic architecture courses has been falling steadily since 2010. In 2014, only 947 students joined the UK register of architects after having completed their studies here.

The newly opened London School of Architecture hopes to circumvent some of the financial problems by offering lower fees. They hope to do so, first, by cutting their own overheads and, second, by offering a work-subsidised fee structure. In the first year, students work three days a week in a practice, for which they are paid a minimum of £12,000. This covers the tuition fees for both years, which are set at £6,000 – so effectively it is 'cost neutral' to study. By the second year they are studying full time, and the London School offers work with a group of 50 London-based practice partners. This system may work well in London where a quarter of the practices are based, but not in other parts of the UK.

Now that the UK government has signalled that university fees may rise to over £9,000 per annum, it will certainly affect the intake of architecture and other creative arts' students as course expenses are already so high.[36] So, given the incentive of lower or no fees and the availability of grants in the EU, it could make financial sense to study outside the UK and then come back to practise here. According to critics,[37] UK students are 'not only paying more but they are getting less'. Many UK students are starting to move to EU universities that compete fiercely for students. The Netherlands, which is less than an hour by air, for example, offers many of its courses, including architecture, in English. The University of Groningen offers Master's programmes under the thematic field of 'Architecture, Urban and Regional Planning' at its Faculty of Spatial Sciences. Not only is the university ranked 83rd in the world in its employability rankings by the *New York Times*, its tuition fees are much more affordable at less than €2,000 per year with reasonable costs of living (and support to pay is available). Even language is not a barrier. The Slavic countries are teaching many courses in English or offer reduced price language courses for foreign students. Some British students feel that studying in the Netherlands or elsewhere in Europe gives them an 'edge' in design and technical areas over those who studied in the UK.

The commodification of education

Whether you stack shelves in the supermarket or become an architect, a university education has become a necessity – in 1950 there were less than 20,000 university students in the UK, whereas now there are a million.[38] The public funding of teaching for the majority of architecture programmes in England effectively ceased after 2011 (as with other subject areas) with funding cuts of over 12 per cent. So universities have been looking at other ways of increasing their income. These measures have impacted on students

98 The autotelic education

and staff. Fundraising tactics include selling off buildings on prime land, increasing student fees by as much as 260 per cent and increasing accommodation costs. Some courses are being funded through corporate means, especially IT – therefore not only does the campus feel different but this kind of 'sponsored' teaching may not be rounded or balanced. Sadly though, this has become a necessity. One friend commented: 'On a recent trip back to my old university, I saw parts of it being transformed into a corporate Disneyland – probably the only way to ensure its survival.'[39]

The UK universities appear to be milking the foreign students who want a British education. One university was in the news because it was offering a course of medical studies at exorbitant fees to foreign students only. The numbers of overseas students applying to UK universities to study architecture, particularly in London, rose by 14 per cent in 2014. It appears that despite the high fees, visa problems and living expenses, foreign students are attracted to the UK, especially London. According to a Chinese architect who studied in London and is now an international high flyer: 'You can't get any better than a London-based architecture education.'[40] In one architecture school that I visited, Chinese students outnumbered the domestic ones, and I was informed that some of the income from the high fees the foreign students were paying was going towards the much-needed renovation and extension of the building. While it may seem fitting that the architecture tuition fees were funding building work, it is sad that universities have to resort to such means to fund essential but non-academic work.

It has been announced that annual tuition fees for foreign students will rise more than the current £15,000. It is not known yet how the influx of overseas students and the income of universities will be affected. But if this lessens the number of overseas students, London will suffer more because between one-fifth and one-third of its students come from abroad, helping the universities make up for the government funding cuts and letting them retain their best teaching staff. Architecture schools where more than 30 per cent of students are from overseas will be affected if demand falls due to high fees. On top of this, the new classification of foreign students as 'immigrants' has resulted in problems for many schools of architecture where a student may wish to do their 'year out' in the UK before proceeding on to Part 2.[41] In 2012–2013, the withdrawal of one university's licence by the Home Office as a 'sponsor' affected many non-EU students because they could not get the Tier 4 (general) student visa, and some architecture students even had to go back or transfer to another university. The difficulty of getting an appropriate visa is a shame because schools of architecture will continue to lose both talented students and the income from fees.

Across the EU where tuition fees are low or non-existent and visa processes are simpler, universities are taking a different kind of action in light of funding cuts. They are merging together in order to share and rationalise resources. Almost 100 mergers have taken place since the beginning of the century. There were eight 'super-universities' or clusters in 2012, 12 in 2013 and 14 in 2014. These academic super-clusters offer advantages of diverse courses for students under one banner while boosting student numbers and achieving a higher profile. Estonia and Denmark[42] were the leaders in this process, with France, Finland and Germany now following their lead. Mergers have also allowed 'super-universities' to lower their fees and attract bright students from abroad.[43]

Some other mergers will see the universities offering architecture courses at reduced fees. In Finland, the Helsinki School of Economics, Helsinki University of Technology and the University of Arts and Design have merged, thus offering students a diverse culture of education that includes collaboration with engineers and economists. So architecture schools in the UK will not only be competing with each other but also with those super-universities on the continent for an ever-smaller share of the student pie. In 2015, UCL (which runs a well-respected architecture school) announced that it was merging with the Institute of Education to make London's largest university of 35,000 students. It appears that such mergers, which offer economies of scale, are a better option than burdening students with more financial liabilities during a significant period of their lives.

International collaborations, which attract both UK and foreign students, are another way of increasing student numbers, diversifying educational outcomes without needing additional buildings or increased fees. Within the EU, there exist student exchange programmes such as the Erasmus, Socrates and the Lifelong Learning Programmes.[44] A few architecture schools in the UK collaborate with foreign schools of architecture through exchange programmes or running a collaborative facility abroad.[45] These choices can be good for a student looking for a school with an international outlook. London Metropolitan University opened architecture schools

100 The autotelic education

in Moscow and Seoul – each of these courses being validated by the London school. This kind of collaboration again offers a unique opportunity for students – for example, one ended up working her year out in Seoul where more work was available than in London.

The education funding cuts have also led to teaching and research funding falling on average by 4 per cent, while capital spending has more than halved. Ironically, universities that focus on research do best, while newer ones, which do more teaching, fare worse. For schools of architecture, demonstrating research is difficult, as much of the practical work carried out by design tutors is not considered as 'serious' research or difficult to describe as a 'methodology' due to its creative and intuitive nature. The other problem is with the increasing numbers of part-time tutors (who may be also running an office); there is simply not enough time to do research, let alone a PhD. As a lecturer commented:

> The difficulty for our part-time or zero hour faculty colleagues is that [they] are too busy juggling their practice and teaching. Zero hours staff have no job security beyond the end of an academic session, and are unlikely to be interested in serving the long-term research ambitions of their employer. Their practice may be world class, but unless they can be rewarded or remunerated for the time it takes to capture and articulate the value of that design-as-research to the widest possible audience, they will not be recognised by the academic community.[46]

The importance of research for the school's reputation and the future prospects of academics are such that having a PhD has become a necessity. For architects having already been through many years of training, to embark on research towards a doctorate is a daunting prospect. Some headway has been made, because one of the key changes in architectural education over the past decade has been the acceptance of design as a legitimate research area in its own right.[47] A few schools of architecture offer a PhD by design or projects, and I hope that this will become the norm for architecture schools if they want their teaching staff to have doctorates.

Design education: purpose and intent

Purely design-focused education is one of the more modern developments of architectural education. In ancient Rome, the subject of architecture included the modern equivalents of construction management, construction engineering, chemical engineering, civil engineering, materials engineering, mechanical engineering, military engineering and urban planning. But studies of technical subjects have gradually been decreased while design time has increased. As seen in the validation documents, RIBA gives great importance to design education: 'Broadly interpreted, design represents the key intellectual and practical skill of an architect; therefore, at least 50 per cent of all assessed work at Part 1 and at Part 2 is to be executed as design studio projects.'[48] The thrust towards design assumes that, given the right sort of teaching, all students will emerge as good designers. However, design is a subjective course dependent upon both the learner and teacher. And so not all students will end up getting good marks or pass because of the bias towards design study – although they may be good in other areas such as theory or technical studies. And even more significant is that the best students may not succeed professionally once out of the academic environment because of the lack of practical knowledge.

Under the pupillage system, the student learnt from their employers, accompanying them to building sites and making notes and drawings – this was used until the 1970s in Scotland. Teaching architecture in the confines of the school building through the unit or studio system was developed at the Architectural Association School of Architecture in London in the 1970s. From there, it spread to a few other architecture schools, in each of which it took different forms according to institutional circumstances and academic aims. The main goal became to offer choice, so each school of architecture started to have many units or studios focused on different projects or design ideologies. Now, owing to an increase in student numbers and catering to the need for giving students free choice, each studio presents their methodology and focus on a 'market' day. Students choose studio units via ballots, and some of the more popular units may have to conduct interviews as well because they have too many applicants.

The 'studio system' of architectural education has been held up as a means of understanding complex and critical problem-solving and for 'thinking like an architect'. According to RIBA, the critique of inadequate focus on the practicalities of construction and delivery is balanced by recognition of the high-level skills of analysis and design development that the academic component of UK architectural education provides. However, some question whether such a

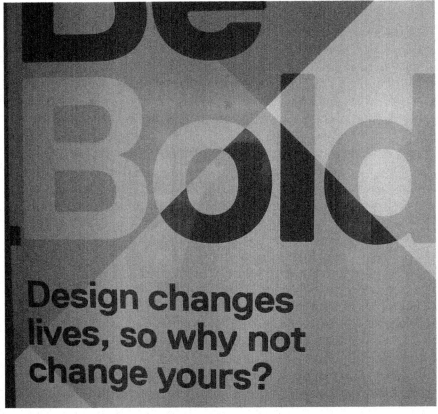

Figure 3.1 Design courses are marketed to appeal to the heart. However, the space and teaching resources needed to teach subjects like architecture make them less financially attractive for universities than others that might need just a lecture theatre or could be even managed online. It has been suggested that universities should have a mix of lucrative courses such as law with the more resource-hungry design courses, so that universities can sustain themselves financially

Source: author.

'general design experience', which includes study of mostly iconic buildings, can be a useful training for real-life practice. In 2002, Wolf Tochtermann, Co-President of the UNESCO/UIA Validation Committee for Architectural Education, remarked:

> Do schools of architecture prepare young architects for a professional life characterised by increasing and diversified demands? What is the relationship today between education and professional practice? Which are the study programmes and curricula that permit the choice of specific streams leading to clearly defined qualification profiles? Will the young architect be trained to dialogue on an equal basis with representatives of other professions actively involved in design, management and renovation in the field of construction? Will he/she be apt to act within the political movement and participate in the political and administrative decision-making that precede the architect's intervention?[49]

It is clear that we are still not ready to answer these questions today as we continue to adjust our architectural education in a reactive and defensive manner. While the rigid stylistic concerns of the Beaux Arts type have become less relevant today, the present studio culture may not offer students a rounded education, including the practical business lessons that would enable a new graduate to launch his or her own practice. Consider also that in practice today the architect may not be the lead in the design project but one within the team. The design studio system does not encourage students to learn about teamwork and collaboration with their co-professionals – instead it continues the old narrative about the 'architect-leader'. Economics, politics and wider planning issues are also touched on half-heartedly or not at all. Further, the units have also been accused of 'promotion of personality cults and specific associated aesthetics'.[50]

In the meantime, technical studies and advocacy are taught collectively (as if they were poor cousins), while design is taught in units – thus creating a separation and a sense of exclusivity for the units. I did not enjoy doing the pages of calculation of indeterminate structures during my architecture studies, but it has inculcated a lifelong appreciation for structures. While I do not think students should be subjected to this level of technical studies any more, a little more rigour in the case of technical studies would be better for all. In the RIBA report published in September 2015, the developer Stuart Lipton stated:

104   The autotelic education

> Architects' rigorous educational training does not include an understanding of the practical implications of how to build. This removes some of the skills required for a successful project and, increasingly, architects and quantity surveyors look for trade contractors to supply these skills. Not only does this add cost but it impacts design quality and in my view the curriculum needs to be changed.[51]

Design-centred teaching just strengthens the position and values of a 'concept architect' and not the 'delivery architect'. It is no wonder that a graduate complained:

> While it is essential that students are encouraged to develop their creative design in their early days at architectural school, they must be educated to be able to react to the realities of practice. The fact that architecture is a practical art and buildings have to work does not seem to have any priority in schools. This is mainly due to the imbalance in the schools of tutors who have had no recent experience – if any – in the reality of practice rather than theory.[52]

RIBA, in particular as the validator of courses, also needs to redefine the twentieth-century role of the architect to fit with twenty-first-century reality[53] given the scale of environmental and technological challenges the younger generation of architects will have to deal with. If the UK is not able to make its own architectural education work, then it is disingenuous for RIBA to validate courses in other countries by using its own criteria as a reference.

The conclusion of the historic 2015 Paris climate change summit will have major impacts on the building industry and design and will affect the future practice of students. But environmental concerns are not universally acknowledged across schools of architecture – only if a particular school or unit specialises in it. Frustrated by the lack of mainstream institutions' interest in sustainability, the Centre for Alternative Technology (CAT) has started its own Part 2 course focused on sustainable architecture and is delivered at CAT's Graduate School of the Environment in Wales, in collaboration with the University of East London. Students spend a month there, learning and working on projects. Although green issues are becoming more important, do such specialised Part 2s offer the 'rounded education' that a student should look for? I believe that all schools and units should be teaching sustainable design, along with technical studies.

This elevation of design over technical studies has given rise to particular problems for year-out students. RIBA's 2014 skills survey of employers and students reported that a total of 86 per cent of employers and 82 per cent of students agreed that students/graduates lack the knowledge to build what they design, and 80 per cent of employers and 73 per cent of students felt that graduates lack the practical skills to practise architecture. Crucially, both sides (79 per cent and 77 per cent) agreed that students should spend more time learning practical matters. Then there is this paradox – while UK students and employers complain about the lack of technical studies experience, UK practices are unable to take on EU graduates despite their superior technical prowess due to a lack of work experience.

Patrik Schumacher, Director of Zaha Hadid Architects, said British architecture students' failure to tackle a tougher scientific agenda was putting them at a competitive disadvantage.[54] 'We need a new skill base,' he said. 'Twenty years ago you could just come in with an art degree and just let your pen flow but now, to have the next level of precision and complexity, that's no longer sufficient.' By decreasing the number of technically able graduates (and not accepting those from outside the UK), we may have forfeited our right to complain about other professions such as engineers and quantity surveyors taking on more responsibilities in a design project.

Engaging with the wider world

Engagement is a crucial part of the architectural practice, and defines the relationship between the architects and their co-professionals, the architects and their clients, and finally the architects and their environment. RIBA validation criteria integrate participation and engagement with design teaching:

- GC5: understanding of the relationship between people and buildings, and between buildings and their environment, and the need to relate buildings and spaces between them to human needs and scale.
- GC6: understanding of the profession of architecture and the role of the architect in society, in particular in preparing briefs that take account of social factors.

106 The autotelic education

Many units work on real design projects that the tutors bring from their offices.[55] For example, in August 2015, architect José Selgas, of the Spanish firm SelgasCano, completed a vaccination and educational centre for the nomadic Turkana people in Kenya along with students of architecture from MIT. During the design process, the architect hoped to 'interrupt the students' dependence on digital technologies'[56] and confront them with more basic questions of habitat and design. The London School proposes a similar scenario where a network of 'host practices' will teach design through participation in real projects but with significant improvement – students will be paid for the work.

In some schools, theory and technical studies are also taught by practitioners, to which they bring their practical knowledge. At the Bath School of Architecture, for example, 85 per cent of the teaching is done by practitioners – the teaching is practice-led. Some practices operate within schools, such as the Design Research Unit at the Welsh School of Architecture and the Architecture Research Unit at London Metropolitan University. They also run units and so offer a chance of not just design but also research experience for the students who join the unit and later the practice.

Learning from practice also ensures evenness in the learning experience of the students if carried out in small teams. Each student will absorb aspects that they are skilled or interested in and be able to collaborate for the final design, just like they would do in real life. Further, it has been suggested that architecture students learn most not from studio critique (crits) but from watching an experienced designer unravelling and resolving a problem on the board.[57] Even within undergraduate teaching there are aspects of practical study such as the 'construction diary' for undergraduates at the University of Westminster where students observe site works and complete an illustrated diary, reflecting on what they have learnt. The PEDR also could become an even better tool if the existing section on reflective learning is extended.[58]

Another route promoted by RIBA is the RIBA Examination in Architecture for Office-Based Candidates, otherwise known as the Office-Based Examination (in short the OBE, perhaps not without a sense of irony). Here, like the London School, students remain in full-time employment and use an in-office mentor and independent tutor to guide them. Learning outcomes and final awards are equivalent to those of full-time courses and the curriculum is laid out as per the RIBA validation. According to RIBA, the programme attracts a diverse range of students at different stages of their studies.

Some enter after getting Part 1 from cognate disciplines such as architectural technology or interior architecture. Some enter at Part 2 to move towards registration, and some come directly from employment. Coursework is self-directed and timescales are flexible, but if starting from Part 1 then the typical completion period is comparable to full-time courses at about six years. Thus, there is flexibility and some financial stability during the study. However, limited numbers of practices have taken up this option to host students.

Live projects

A popular area of engaged learning is 'live projects' where students get involved with communities in actual projects. These are usually community projects, instigated (and sometimes managed) by the community. The design units come as stakeholders in the process. Live projects form a way of connecting to people directly without the need for formal studios located inside the school – it is the classroom outside. There have been many educators in the past that looked to learning within the community or within nature as the most powerful tools for practical learning experiences, such as Rabindranath Tagore of India and Tsunesaburo Makiguchi of Japan. The original proponent of this kind of architectural education has been the Rural Studio at Auburn University in Alabama, USA, conceived by the late Samuel 'Sambo' Mockbee. The students and tutors of the Rural Studio have built more than 80 houses and civic projects and received several awards since their initiation in 1995.

Many other such initiatives operate now in the UK, South Africa, Australia, India and other countries. At Sheffield University, students work on live projects with a range of clients including local community groups, charities, health organisations and regional authorities. 'In every case, the project is real, happening in real time with real people.'[59] In China, the Pritzker winning architect Wang Shu and other artists are taking this idea to a radical extreme – Shu is not only building an entire village of rammed earth and local stone, but will be moving his entire office and also building an architecture school there. There the students will be working on live projects and focusing on rural life. In the UK, the 'Resourceful Architect' competition for students organised by the RSA in 2011 showed that live projects within a curriculum were very popular, but currently such projects are not recognised as part of the PEDR – hence the uptake of such studio work has been limited.

Figure 3.2 The 'recycled' office of charity Oasis, London, by Benjamin Marks and Matt Atkins. This project received the first ever *RIBAJ* MacEwen Award in 2016, an award that sets out to recognise architecture for the common good, i.e. for social and ethical aims. Interestingly, the award – named after Malcolm and Anni MacEwen, respectively, a former *RIBAJ* editor and conservation-minded architect-planner in the post-war years – is given to the project rather than an individual, recognising the collaborative nature of such schemes

Source: Benjamin Marks and Matt Atkins.

The autotelic education   109

An example of subversive and autotelic action might be the work of former students at London Metropolitan University, Benjamin Marks and Matt Atkins, who found out that a Segal-method former office structure was scheduled for the skip. So they dismantled it into its constituent parts and moved it to a playground where a charity was looking for offices. The simple constructive logic of its original design became the key to the material's reuse, allowing it to be cleanly separated and reused again in a new configuration and setting. Ben and Matt covered different roles – demolition and removals, construction, designers (including securing of statutory approvals) and managing the reconstruction process. Situated within the playground, the building comprises a new indoor play space, a staff office, a kitchen, a veranda and ancillary functions. The new building has enabled the playground to be open more often, while enabling the charity to have additional staff and facilities. Ben says:

> The project was my first building and I was able to learn a lot from it, both in terms of construction, and the whole process of actually getting something built. It has led to further projects such as my most recent building, The Green Room, which is a neighbourhood restaurant.[60]

Students need the encouragement and opportunities to work on projects like this. Ben and Matt's experience was a good learning experience, leading on to more work upon graduation. But when students do not know enough about the local community, such experiences may not be useful. Understanding and working in local contexts take time – they cannot be done in ten-day overseas trips. I remember sitting in one crit where a student with complete innocence presented a building set in a slum of Delhi inspired by Zaha Hadid's designs. Siting 'live projects' within local communities would also enable the students to work for longer with the community and get more work, as Ben and Matt did. I believe that while exotic experiences can be valuable for understanding global issues such as scarcity, inequality and displacement (and humanitarian crisis), they need to be set out more sensitively and be given more time – both for the visit and for the design process.

Creating good architecture schools

In his acceptance speech for the Honorary Fellowship of RIBA in February 2015, the late Dalibor Vesely said: 'Architecture is made

110 The autotelic education

not only in the offices where there is often very little time to explore and invent ... some of the most interesting recent contributions to architectural innovation come from better schools of architecture.' It is true that there is time to explore, push the boundaries and stretch one's imagination at schools of architecture – time that will not be available easily when practising it for real. Someone has described the architecture school as a 'playground'. The time at school is best spent on flexing and building those creative and inquisitive muscles. So that may be the reason why most design studies do not think to include learning about ordinary everyday buildings such as housing, schools or hospitals (or retrofit, which provides 57 per cent of architects' work in the EU) – because these are felt to be not exciting or ambitious. But having designed fantastical buildings during their academic life and then moving to a work experience of being 'CAD monkeys', cutting and pasting windows on a building façade because they are deemed too risky to work on real projects, can be a hugely disappointing descent into reality for year-out and recent graduates.

As Terry Farrell (himself a designer of iconic buildings) said after the publication of his eponymous review in 2014, we need to get better at designing the 'good ordinary', not just the 'haute couture' architecture. This educational objective is important for architecture because the architect's entire work is practised in the arena where people live and work. The press coverage given to high-profile practices and education's focus on the design of large buildings encourage students to believe that there is only one kind of good architecture – the iconic public building. The everyday good that should be expected of decent architectural education has been lost with the importance attached to design teaching within units, especially those led by the ones feted by the press. It may be that, with such an approach towards architectural education, students will be able to think creatively and collaboratively, globally and strategically, about the production of space and the way in which people live in it. Things may be changing, because a number of President's Medals went to students with projects in regeneration, schools or housing, although the top Silver Medal went to a much grander scheme for a city.

Good design schools also work with cognate professionals. Cross-disciplinary studio work for students will be of great benefit later. There are architecture schools that collaborate with or are housed in buildings with other fine arts such as jewellery making, silver-smithing, photography, etc. But doing so pigeonholes architecture as an 'arts' course and propagates the romantic myth of the artist-architect.

Today, more than ever, both larger and smaller projects need input from science and technology. So architecture schools should be collaborating with our co-professionals' subjects such as engineering and surveying, and even the scientific and economic world. This is not to diminish the design aspect but to lift it from merely being a 'utilitarian art' to a realm of higher and real practice. After all, RIBA Gold Medal winner Peter Zumthor's attention to materials and making as well as his technical skills (he also studied industrial design at Pratt) complemented an inherent creative skill. Recognising a gap, a new school of architecture will be starting in 2016 at the University of Reading. Like the London School, it will be collaborating with architectural practices. But the Reading School's arrangements will be about internal collaboration also. They intend to use the university's existing 'connections across the built environment sector (in subjects such as environmental engineering, urban design and sustainable cities), to enable that their students gain as much practical [and technical] experience as possible before they enter the workplace'.[61]

So a more radical arrangement of the studio structure might be a reverse situation where students would choose their technical and theory studies and focus on these in small groups while design could be taught in large classes. In this way, the technical and theory focus will be able to direct the design detail and outcome. Also the technical studies will be much more integrated into the design process than having mass technical lessons and small design units where technical studies appear to be 'add-ons'. Also, learning design among others instead of design teaching in studio silos would encourage an interchange of ideas. This would also reduce the stylistic domination and perceived superiority of some units over others and encourage students to come up with their own styles and ideas. The technological revolution has had the biggest impact on learning and teaching, and now the student has also acquired the freedom to learn from any location by going online. And we have to be open to the possibility that, in the future, all learning – even design – will be carried out digitally, and students need to prepare for this. It may be difficult to predict, but I do wonder if we are foreseeing the slow demise of traditional schools of architecture by bringing back the kind of architectural education that was practised in the past, as apprenticeship within the workplace.

Learning by making is also something schools could encourage. The Frank Lloyd Wright School of Architecture based outside Scottsdale, in Arizona, is a special school that only gained accreditation in 1992

112 The autotelic education

after being set up by Wright in 1932. Here students are encouraged to come with their tuxedos (or evening dresses), sleeping bag and cooking equipment. For the seven months that they study for their M Arch, they have to live in the homes they build themselves. When I visited in 1995, I was taken to see the large numbers of impressive structures that present and past students had constructed. Some had salvaged pieces from previous homes to build entirely new homes, while others were inhabiting remodelled existing structures – but all had to build in order to learn. As one student said:

> I was learning by doing ... when I arrived in 1997, it was as an apprentice to a working architecture practice. After graduating, I went into other architecture firms to make an immediate contribution compared to students in other schools who had only learned theory.[62]

Schools of architecture will also do well to offer modules on basic business skills. There is always the 'hidden contract' in employment, according to Charles Handy, that requires business and soft skills. Some of the atrociously written application letters for jobs probably arise from the jargon-laden language used during crits (see Chapter 2), as students forget how to write clearly and simply. This then carries on later to how they talk to clients and other co-professionals who are unable to understand what is being said.[63] Other skills that are useful include handwriting (still relevant, as site and meeting notes are often handwritten and must be legible – 59 per cent of employers look out for writing skills[64]) and typing skills (very useful for today's digital world), note taking, letter writing and observation. Around 70 per cent of employers saw hand drawing as a core skill, despite the advent of digital technology and CGI, yet architecture schools persist in having computer drawings from their students, not to mention the poor cousin of hand drawing the 'sketch-up'. The *RIBA Journal* celebrates hand drawing through its 'Eyeline' competitions that began in 2013, many of which are won by students of architecture. The skill and ability to think independently and conduct self-directed research are also of great importance to the autotelic learner.

Schools of architecture are content to continue the myth of the architect-hero with 'radical' or 'disruptive' ideas who saves the world because it helps them to keep going. While it is good to inspire young people, it is not a good idea to tell them that architecture alone can save the world. In the academic world, apart from the jargon widely

Figure 3.3 The Frank Lloyd Wright School of Architecture, Taliesin West
Source: Vallari Talapatra Ranjan.

114   The autotelic education

DO-IT-YOURSELF ARCHITECTURAL DIALOGUE

COMPOSE 40,000 IMPRESSIVE SENTENCES. SELECT ONE PHRASE FROM EACH COLUMN TO FORM GOBBLEDYGOOK STATEMENTS THAT SOUND PROFOUND.

	COLUMN A	COLUMN B	COLUMN C	COLUMN D
1	One might say	the massing of major elements	must utilize and be functionally interwoven with	the sophisticated design solution
2	Aesthetically speaking	the introduction of brutalism	maximizes the real probability of cost overruns for	the anticipated degree of human ambience
3	On the other hand	the treatment of the main façade	adds specific critical path events to	the acuteness of the conflict gradient
4	Based upon inter-disciplinary considerations	the initial stage of conceptual development	necessitates that urgent considerations be made of	the pragmatics of value engineering
5	With sensitive respect for human scale	the by-product of repetitive space articulation	requires exhaustive trade-off study to arrive at	the final quantitative analysis
6	Indubitably	the life-cycle cost control	is further compounded by taking into account	the evolution of performance specifications
7	Above and beyond plebian comfort objectives	the environmental impact analysis	presents extremely synergistic challenges to	the philosophy of commonality and standardization
8	Beyond the horizon of the human intellect	energy conservation regulations	recognizes the critical necessity to subtract from	the study of true fecundity in the state of the art
9	Architecturally thinking	the structural dynamic analysis	imposes smothering constraints upon	the creation of an immortal monument to posterity
10	In the final rationalization	the internal use adjacencies and circulation	adds overriding three dimensional constraints to	the final abortion

As a bonus service to our friends and clients, we thought it appropriate to provide the above "Do-it-yourself Architectural Dialogue" chart.

Those of you who are not school-trained in architecture will find this invaluable in conversing with designers and governmental authorities. Just think of any four-digit number (say, 2447), consult your handy chart, and read off the similarly numbered phrases from Columns A, B, C, and D. I.e. – 2447 = "Aesthetically speaking the initial stage of conceptual development necessitates that urgent considerations be made of the philosophy of commonality and standardization."

Never mind what it means, just use it and watch the way you stop conversation. You can compose entire speeches or profound reports just by using varied number combinations.

As you become more proficient in its use, you may wish to experiment with varying column sequences, i.e. BADC, CBAD, etc. However, these advanced configurations are not recommended for beginners, as they do require sophisticated dexterity with punctuation.

Figure 3.4 DIY architectural dialogue

Source: courtesy of Harvard University.

used in crits, every lecture becomes a polemic, every list becomes a manifesto (yes, I heard that so many times that I began to think I was living in a communist country), and students buy into the idea of the 'revolution' and 'ambition' of the 'architect-hero'. Not every student will create a revolution or change the world. It may be a better strategy to encourage the student to become an independent thinker and even a sceptic. According to the architect Liz Diller, education is about pushing people to analyse, to examine and to break the rules. She thinks that the most important thing she can teach her students is to continue investigating because architecture is always evolving – it isn't canonical.[65] Bernard Tschumi also concurs: 'Never take anything for granted. Never accept what people tell you the solution is. Always start with a question.'[66]

Tsunesaburo Makiguchi believed that the purpose of education was to prepare students for the real world. Working life is, of course, never as exciting as the academic world of make believe, and the disappointment of ordinary design may be depressing. And practices are not willing to waste their precious resources on training someone armed with a glamorous portfolio of unbuildable shiny and scary structures. Many leave architecture after having waited tables instead of finding work as year-out students. Perhaps they wanted to do something else anyway. But for those who are ready and willing, students and tutors working with the community will aid them in this quest – anything from live projects to community engagement and consultation. Teaching is in a way an antithesis to the creative process – being based on authority, reasoning and submission of evidence – so design teaching for creative thinking must encourage autonomy, self-direction and intuitive problem-solving. As Mockbee reminds us: 'If architecture is going to nudge, cajole, and inspire a community to challenge the status quo into making responsible changes, it will take the subversive leadership of academics and activists who keep reminding students of the profession's responsibilities.'[67]

However, we have to end with the old chestnut of poor pay, which the reader might have noticed has been an ongoing conclusion in everything we have touched upon. A student careers website warns: 'Contracted working hours may be 9am to 5pm, Monday to Friday, but it is not uncommon for architects to work long hours, including evenings and weekends.'[68] Unless pay and work conditions are improved for architecture graduates, no amount of tweaking of the course, funding or delivery will change the situation. In October 2015,[69] it was announced that UK ministers are working to release huge tracts of anonymised data about a subject's earning potential that will allow future students to compare and choose subjects according to their earning potential. Undisputedly architecture will compare poorly with other professions – this will only increase the elitism associated with architecture studies, as only those who can afford a low salary upon graduation will study it.

Three qualities of the autotelic learner: failure, focus and flexibility

The autotelic learner is a good learner, throughout life. There is growing evidence that character traits such as resilience, persistence, optimism and courage actively contribute to improved academic

116 The autotelic education

grades. Interestingly, medical students have a biomedical test that determines their fitness to study a subject so demanding. It may help if architecture perhaps also should follow suit as studying it is not for the faint hearted (as evinced by the 'Selfie a day of a student, bleary and teary eyed).[70] There are many soft skills that students will find useful during practice, but these cannot be taught – they can only be learnt by observation and experience. If architectural education were to be more autotelic, then it would seek to ensure that students become more independent as soon as possible. Therefore, it is important that those teaching the students also talk about their own learning experience and, in particular, three things that they may shy away from discussing with their students – failure, focus and flexibility.

Failure is held up as a negative word, but equally it is a word laden with opportunities. From failure can be learnt many qualities including resilience and risk taking. According to Matthew Syed:

> Youngsters who are taught to think about failure in a more positive light not only become more creative, but more resilient, too. They regard their mess-ups not as reasons to give up, but as intriguing and educative. They engage with these failures, learn from them, and, by implication, develop new insights, and ever-deeper curiosity.[71]

A design college in the USA[72] held a new exhibition about failure in design that ran until January 2016. It was called 'Permission to Fail'. The curator asked a group of 50 well-known designers and illustrators to send in their 'mess-ups', rough drafts and preliminary sketches so that viewers could see that failure was not an obstacle to success.

Failure and risk taking should be discussed at architecture schools as part of creative thinking. These two aspects of creativity emerged in the account I heard in 2015:

> Twenty years ago, I was straight out of architecture school, working for Foster + Partners, completing my Part 3. Then came along this amazing project – something that had never been built before. It required new ways of thinking and designing combining the traditional with modern requirements, innovative engineering solutions, sourcing of materials from two different countries, one of which was a communist stronghold; shipping the materials to another country in another continent where 20,000 craftsmen worked in a specially built workshop near the docks. The finished pieces were then shipped back to the UK and then each piece was

The autotelic education   117

attached to the other on site like Lego blocks. I was only 27 then, but my design education had taught me to take risks and I had also learnt a lot while working on big projects with Fosters. I felt confident to do this – so confident that I sold my house in South London and my wife and I moved to a flat closer to the site. I was told that I could come back when the project was finished so I took at three-year sabbatical from work. I overcame many hurdles including statutory permissions for the unique type of construction and finding funding for the project. The project attracted the attention of many community volunteers who came to work on it. Now the project has won several awards and has become an important tourist attraction with visitors from all over the world. It has also changed planning rules in the borough, revitalised the area economically and socially, bringing businesses back to what was a disused car park. I now run my own award-winning practice.[73]

You may not have guessed the name of the building or its self-effacing architect I am quoting – it is the Shrinarayan Hindu temple in Neasden and Amrish Patel. The story of the construction of the Neasden temple is really another book, but what fascinated me was Amrish's frank and enduring compliment to architectural education he received in the late 1980s and also how his academic experience taught him to take risks and not be afraid of failure.

But the commodification of education has had another unintended consequence by removing or minimising risk-taking in order to reduce failure. This has come about through an uneasy relationship of the student as a 'consumer' and the teacher as a 'service provider'.[74] I had my own taste of this when some students demanded that I compensate them for the 45 minutes I had spent photocopying 550 pages of their group submission work while they waited. That they ought to have done this copying themselves as part of the requirement, or that they could have spent that waiting time more productively or even that I was saving them money, did not of course occur to them. The onset of the 'litigious culture' within universities (along with schools, hospitals and other public sector services) has created an environment where both students and academics are afraid of risk-taking and experimentation, with a negative consequence for the quality of the learning experience. The rise of the 'fragile learner' where students are offered counselling (or students are ready to sue the teacher) if questions are too stressful or too technical is another symptom of the fear of failure. Martin Seligman, the US psychology professor who has studied

Figure 3.5 Shrinarayan Hindu temple, Neasden, London, was completed in just two years and cost £12 million. It is made of nearly 3,000 tonnes of Bulgarian limestone and 2,000 tonnes of Italian marble, which was first shipped to India to be carved by a team of 1,526 sculptors. The process of building the first new Hindu temple outside India, using not only the latest technology with bolt-on parts and prefabrication but also combining traditional craftsmanship with ritualistic needs, was a complex process

Source: author.

The autotelic education 119

resilience extensively, concluded that a resilient character helps one to think more flexibly and realistically, be more creative and ward off depression and anxiety. Resilient people understand that the course of learning has plenty of setbacks but that those can be overcome. According to philosopher Julian Baggini, 'a survey of human resources showed that more than 90 per cent of employers believed that the employee's ability to cope with change and uncertainty will determine their likelihood of being hired in five years' time'.[75]

The current diversity of studio units may give students a choice but it does not leave them with a focus. As it stands, academic life provides the student with a smorgasbord of likely projects they may encounter later, along with history and theory; and a smattering of technical studies. Architectural education must provide not only a way of helping a student broaden their horizons and absorb all that is given to them, but also the ability to then narrow down and choose what they would like to concentrate on. The ability to 'scan first and then focus' continually is what would stand the autotelic learner in good stead when they start to practise. Marcus Aurelius explained more graphically: 'Always look at the whole of a thing. Find out what it is that makes an impression on you, then open it up and dissect it into cause, matter, purpose, and the length of time before it must end.'[76] But it is important that the focus should come from the student and not be directed by the teacher. This way the learning will be internalised – therefore autotelic. Being focused also helps in practical matters such as the ability to study, do self-directed research and manage time and money.

In a complex and chaotic world, autotelic learners are determined but also flexible – taking advantage of the opportunities as they come about. While they almost always have a point of view about a situation, they are capable of shifting to other perspectives to see what they can find. Another way of saying this is that good learners seem to understand that solutions are relative, not absolute. Flexibility is a key quality for team-working, especially with co-professionals who often don't see eye to eye with architects but are increasingly becoming important parts of the team. The image of a 'diva architect' throwing their weight around is a thing of the past, and soft skills needed to persuade and lead are more important now. Furthermore, in today's global market with diverse cultures within international time zones, understanding the concept of flexibility will be a key factor in determining success.

We have to remind ourselves that schools of architecture could be hives of creativity and innovation given the extraordinary talent that comes to them. According to Bernard Tschumi:

I think architecture is something quite extraordinary because it's still in the making. There's in no way the feeling that it is not still in front of us, so places like schools are quite extraordinary because they are really the places that prepare the brew of what architecture will become tomorrow. The young faculty has generally more energy and invention than the practice. It makes for fantastic people to work with and to develop what will become, by necessity, the architecture and the cities of the next generation.[77]

How our future architects are being taught about these changes, how they must relate to society and place, and how they will work are issues that academics and students must explore with new eyes. The future of architecture is in the hands of these students.

Notes

1 Both sons had problematic personalities. The elder, who used to assault his wife and child, was eventually jailed for fraud and theft, and disinherited. That son also had a son by his wife's sister who lived with them – it is this grandson that Soane tried to attract to architecture. Soane's younger son suffered from poor health and was estranged from his parents.
2 Of course the desire to do the opposite of what the parent might want is also part of human nature.
3 A study by the Institute of Fiscal Studies shows that Chinese (76 per cent) and Indian (67 per cent) populations are the likeliest to attend university, while White British (33 per cent) are at the bottom of that list. www.independent.co.uk/student/news/chinese-indian-and-black-african-children-more-likely-to-attend-university-in-england-than-white-a6730411.html (accessed November 2015).
4 https://en.wikipedia.org/wiki/List_of_architecture_schools (accessed May 2014).
5 http://archinect.com/people/cover/21851602/keith-carlson (accessed October 2014).
6 https://en.wikipedia.org/wiki/List_of_architecture_schools (accessed September 2014).
7 www.architectsjournal.co.uk/students/essay-so-you-want-to-be-an-architect/8686617.fullarticle (accessed September 2015).
8 Cartledge (2014, pp. 22–3).
9 The administration charge is subject to annual review, and any updated charge is posted on www.architecture.com; these will supersede the sum stated in these procedures. This applies equally to UK and international schools.
10 More details can be found on the RIBA website.
11 Personal communication.

The autotelic education 121

12 www.oxfordconference2008.co.uk/1958conference.pdf (accessed December 2015).
13 The conclusion of the 1958 Oxford Conference on Architectural Education was that the entry into the architectural profession had to be almost exclusively via an academic route, though periods of work experience were woven into it.
14 www.wg.aegee.org/ewg/bologna.htm (accessed September 2015).
15 'Why do women leave architecture?', RIBA, 2003.
16 'Architecture and race', CABE, 2004.
17 www.bdonline.co.uk/comment/opinion/why-you-need-to-go-to-an-elite-university-to-win-the-stirling-prize/5078403.article (accessed November 2015). A reader responded: 'Let's not kid ourselves, the education system today does not favour the best and brightest, it is riddled with bias based on connections, class, money, etc. Unfortunately, architecture is full of people scratching each other's backs, not just in schools but in the industry and its bodies/associations.'
18 www.dur.ac.uk/school.health/phase1.medicine/career (accessed March 2016).
19 www.theguardian.com/artanddesign/2013/jun/27/pressure-builds-change-schools-architecture (accessed December 2014).
20 www.nhscareers.nhs.uk/explore-by-career/doctors/training-to-become-a-doctor/undergraduate-medical-education/financial-support-for-students-on-degree-courses-in-medicine (accessed December 2014).
21 http://people.bath.ac.uk/absaw/files/Preliminary%20Report%20-%20Pathways%20and%20Gateways.pdf (accessed July 2015).
22 www.bdonline.co.uk/news/riba-agrees-biggest-shake-up-in-architectural-education-for-50-years/5074559.article?PageNo=1&SortOrder=dateadded&PageSize=50#comments (accessed March 2015).
23 www.bdonline.co.uk/comment/debate/are-schools-of-architecture-letting-students-down?/5014816.article (accessed March 2011).
24 Now referred to as Professional Practical Experience (PPE). www.pedr.co.uk/FAQ#Top (accessed September 2014).
25 'Spain's constant churn of employees raises questions about productivity', *Financial Times*, 5 August 2015.
26 www.arb.org.uk/files/files/ARB-Fee-Schedule.pdf (accessed April 2016).
27 www.dezeen.com/2013/02/22/report-unpaid-architecture-internships-says-riba-president-angela-brady (accessed November 2014).
28 Ibid.
29 Sutton Trust research report, 'What makes great teaching?', November 2014.
30 www.legislation.gov.uk/ukia/2016/3/pdfs/ukia_20160003_en.pdf (accessed December 2015).
31 Many student loan companies have started up in the wake of this issue.
32 www.studentloanrepayment.co.uk/portal/page?_pageid=93,6678490&_dad=portal&_schema=PORTAL (accessed December 2015).
33 The Royal College of Art (a postgraduate-only university) in 2015 gave out 204 bursaries worth £10,000 each after other universities could not take up the government's offer.

122 The autotelic education

34 www.bbc.co.uk/news/magazine-32821678 (accessed July 2015).

35 www.theguardian.com/education/2014/sep/30/tuition-fees-bonanza-for-one-per-cent-danny-dorling?CMP=fb_gu (accessed February 2015).

36 www.independent.co.uk/news/uk/politics/budget-2015-live-emergency-uk-universities-will-be-allowed-to-raise-fees-beyond-9000-10375910.html (accessed July 2015).

37 www.architectsjournal.co.uk/culture/rosbottom-students-are-not-only-paying-more-they-are-getting-less/8686733.fullarticle (accessed August 2015).

38 Includes foreign and post-graduate students – statistics from www.hesa.ac.uk (accessed September 2015).

39 Personal communication.

40 'Wai Tang returns', *Network Magazine*, pp. 40–1, University of Westminster, 2015.

41 www.telegraph.co.uk/education/universityeducation/11053743/Foreign-students-should-not-be-classed-as-immigrants.html (accessed December 2014).

42 Estonia cut the numbers of its universities down from 49 to 24, while Denmark came down from 12 to eight.

43 In 2013–2014, admission fees to a super-university were fixed at €183 for an undergraduate degree, €254 for a Master's degree and €388 for a PhD degree. These fees are much lower than in the UK.

44 More than 4,000 higher institutions participate in these exchange programmes across 33 countries. In 2012–2013, 270,000 students took part, the most popular destinations being Spain, Germany and France. Now secondary school students are also being included.

45 While London schools may be opening facilities abroad, regional schools of architecture are opening schools in London – a city that may as well be considered a 'foreign territory' by them.

46 www.linkedin.com/pulse/commodification-architectural-education-sumita-sinha?trk=mp-reader-card (accessed March 2016).

47 Fraser (2013).

48 www.architecture.com/files/ribaprofessionalservices/education/validation/ribavalidationcriteriafromseptember2011parts1,23.pdf (accessed January 2015).

49 www.aij.or.jp/jpn/aijedu/Systeme_eng.pdf (accessed September 2015).

50 'So you want to study architecture?', *AJ*, 24 July 2015.

51 'Client and architect: Developing the essential relationship' was launched at a RIBA reception on 15 September 2015.

52 www.architectsjournal.co.uk/how-architecture-education-is-limiting-students/8643685.article (accessed November 2015).

53 Building Futures, RIBA study.

54 www.bdonline.co.uk/patrik-schumacher-britains-supremacy-at-risk-because-students-shun-maths/5070888.article (accessed September 2014).

55 Architecture, along with other creative subjects, is recognising the value of working on 'live projects'. This website documents such academic projects across the world in diverse creative subjects, using different forms of funding and engagement: http://liveprojectsnetwork.org (accessed April 2016).

The autotelic education 123

56 http://www.architecturalrecord.com/articles/7996-konokono-vaccination-center?v=preview (accessed December 2015)

57 www.ribaj.com/intelligence/how-do-we-learn-to-be-architects (accessed November 2015).

58 Schon (1991, pp. 79–104).

59 www.liveprojects.org (accessed March 2016).

60 Personal communication.

61 www.bdonline.co.uk/5078737.article?origin=BDdaily (accessed November 2015).

62 'The great outdoors', *Blueprint*, issue 342, p. 160.

63 A surprising picture is painted by the Organisation of Economic Co-operation and Development (OECD) that the UK is notable for the fact that despite high proportions of people with university or college degrees, there has not been a parallel increase in skills such as literacy – well below other top-performing nations.

64 RIBA Skills Survey Report 2014, London, RIBA, 2015.

65 www.designboom.com/architecture/liz-diller-interview-ds-r-11-27-2014 (accessed December 2014).

66 www.architectural-review.com/old/film/the-ar-interviews/interview-with-bernard-tschumi/8669431.fullarticle (accessed March 2016).

67 Wigglesworth and Till (1998, p. 74).

68 www.prospects.ac.uk/job-profiles/architect (accessed September 2014).

69 www.independent.co.uk/news/education/education-news/students-to-assess-earnings-potential-of-different-courses-with-government-data-a6698966.html (accessed October 2015). Surprisingly, this article has had no comments at all from readers, considering its potential effect on the choice of study subjects at universities.

70 http://thetab.com/us/2016/05/06/took-selfie-day-last-month-architecture-degree-4479 (accessed April 2016).

71 Syed (2015).

72 www.mountida.edu/events/permission-to-fail (accessed November 2015).

73 Interview with Amrish Patel.

74 www.theguardian.com/higher-education-network/2015/dec/18/my-students-have-paid-9000-and-now-they-think-they-own-me (accessed March 2016).

75 'Should we cultivate resilience?', *Financial Times Weekend Magazine*, 4 October 2014.

76 Aurelius (2004, p. 159).

77 www.architectural-review.com/old/film/the-ar-interviews/interview-with-bernard-tschumi/8669431.fullarticle (accessed March 2016).

4 The autotelic architect
Practising architecture in a changing world

In Chapter 1, I wrote about the complex problem of 'doing more with less, faster' and the inequalities that affect every country around the globe. Consider that between 1900 and 2008, world population quadrupled to over 7 billion, while GDP per capita increased six-fold. But despite this 'growth' in GDP, almost a billion people do not have enough to eat, and just under one-half of the world's population lives in absolute poverty. Rapid climate change and man-made violence are destroying the planet and lives.[1] An estimated 1.2 billion people – 17 per cent of the global population – did not have access to electricity in 2013, and 6–8 million people died from water-related issues. Economic growth has not removed inequality but reinforced it. According to Fritjof Capra, these are systemic problems, i.e. they are interconnected and interdependent, so they cannot be separated and solved in isolation. He calls for an 'extremely broad view and [for us to] see our cultural situation in the context of human cultural revolution'.[2] This is also true for architecture, for example, Modernism and Post-Modernism were not exclusively architectural movements – all sections of society were influenced by them, and they arose as a product of those times.

Environmental challenges as a product of 'faster' are multiform – ranging from extreme climatic changes and rising pollution to uncontrolled and rapid urbanisation, as discussed earlier. As our need for homes rises, more people are at risk from rising seas due to homes and cities being closer to coastlines than before. Some four million residential properties in England currently sit on floodplains and, despite warnings, large-scale building in such areas has continued. In fact, according to the UK Committee on Climate Change, housing in areas where flooding is likely has grown at a rate of 1.2 per cent per year since 2011, while the building of residential properties in areas

126 The autotelic architect

of low risk has risen by just 0.7 per cent over the same period. Many African cities (and mega cities), for example, are at risk in a similar way.

Capra encourages us to see these issues as opening up debate and as predecessors of opportunity. He lists a variety of negative social factors such as a sense of alienation, violent crime and religious cultism as indicators of positive changes yet to come.[3] Looking at our current problems with inequality leading to alienation, different types of crime including cyber crime and the rise of religious fundamentalism, we may surmise that if his ideas can be considered valid, then the optimism of 'changing these poisons into medicine'[4] can also hold true. The theory of cyclical change in various forms has been propounded by various Occidental philosophers, including Arnold Toynbee and Vilfredo Pareto, and through many Oriental philosophical strands. Arnold Toynbee's *A Study of History*[5] describes how civilisations face challenges from first the environment and later challenges from internal and external aggressors. The nature of responses to these threats determines the civilisation's fate. Examining the employment levels of architects, we see that those have fluctuated rather than grown steadily as one would expect, while our workloads have fallen. But again, where there has been a recession, architects along with others have suffered, and where there has been a boom, architects have prospered along with others. So if these have been happening historically and architecture and architects have survived, then there is no need to fear but to embrace the opportunities that arise.

We have examined the Victorian era, during which architecture as a profession emerged alongside a remarkable profusion of engineering advances. But whereas engineering continues to flourish, architecture has been declining in social importance. (Even the Duke of Edinburgh remarked: 'Everything that wasn't invented by God was invented by an engineer.'[6]) At first glance, the scale and type of effects of climate change may appear to require intervention and solutions from engineers and scientists only, rather than architects and town planners. For instance, the large-scale engineering interventions in the Earth's climatic system to stop or decrease global warming include Heath Robinsonesque techniques such as sunlight being reflected away from the Earth using huge mirrors, cloud seeding to make rainfall on drought-hit areas, creating man-made mountains to attract rain and carbon capture using algae. But these quick-fix

Figure 4.1 A sixth floating accommodation vessel arrived in Lerwick, Shetland, in 2014 to house 400 additional construction workers at the Sullom Voe Shetland Gas Plant. Such floating accommodation has been used as five-star floating hotels with full facilities, as worker accommodation barges, as floating prisons for governments but, particularly, as onsite accommodation for the offshore wind, oil and gas industries. Some of these have a transfer platform for safe access to working platforms straight from the vessel

Source: author.

128 The autotelic architect

and large-scale solutions may have unintended dangers, apart from being expensive and slow. It may be more appropriate for architects, scientists and engineers to work together to create small, targeted and integrated solutions for problems, rather than carpet bombing geo-engineering solutions.

Solutions need to be multiform because so are the challenges. The autotelic architect's response in the face of societal changes will be towards more sustainable, collaborative and open interventions – both in built forms and practice. There are many means to do this now, and more are opening up. For instance, digital technologies are improving and becoming a way of sharing and collaboration. So there exist plenty of small-scale interventions within the gift of the architect, as they can not only design but also have the ability to be interpreters of 'fuzzy logic' and 'soft' data, more so than scientists and engineers. From individual homes to cities, from local to global, there are all sizes and types of buildings that continue to need the input of architects and enable them to make a positive contribution, globally and locally.

In this chapter, we revisit these dilemmas presented earlier and see in what form the architect can have role to play in our chaotic, complex age. For instance, 2014's New Climate Economy report argued that better urban design, sustainable transport and building energy efficiency could help offset the negative effects of climate change, while contributing positively to the economy. The three main societal themes arising from 'more with less, faster' that offer opportunities for architects, especially smaller practices, concern these aspects:

- Challenges of climate change and opportunities;
- Ageing and healthy cities;
- Urbanisation and city planning.

Challenges of climate change and opportunities

The subject of climate change has been a double-edged sword for architects – we have to design buildings but our buildings one way or the other will release greenhouse gases. Buildings can trade carbon emissions but, in reality, there can be no absolute zero-carbon structures unless you forgo your electrical appliances or plant an awful lot of trees to make up for the carbon emitted.[7] All building materials come with hidden embodied energy costs. The American Institute of Architects National Government Advocacy Team's 2006 report states that 'the largest source of greenhouse gas emissions and energy consumption in [the USA], as well as around the world, is buildings. Buildings account for an estimated 48 per cent of all greenhouse emissions.'[8] In particular, use of coal-fired energy production remains the largest source of CO_2, the main greenhouse gas responsible for climate change, with China being the largest emitter, the USA second, followed by the EU.[9] At present, we have the capability to design low-energy homes and there has been a lot of research into sustainable building techniques. But perhaps we have reached a plateau where, unless this research is applied practically on a large scale, we are not able to test the benefits of it and carry out further research. It won't be enough to design one single green building, we will have to now 'green' our cities too.

Given that the existing carbon sink is likely to lead to up to two degrees of global temperature increase anyway and the 'world's climate about to enter "unchartered territory" as it passes 1°C of warming as of November 2015',[10] many are already confronting problems of rising water or flooding in places such as the USA and Italy. Flood-resilient homes, houses on stilts and even floating accommodation are already designed and used in the Netherlands. Some 50 or so amphibious houses have now been built around the world, including one in the lower ninth ward of New Orleans. The Dutch have been at the forefront of this kind of architecture, given that one-quarter of their reclaimed landmass lies below sea level. Following the 2011 tsunami, Japanese and Italian architects and planners have been collaborating on the mitigation of risks from rising sea levels. In the USA, climate change scientists are presenting states with a score card on climate preparedness and what each state could do to prepare for the climate change adaptation.[11] So far, as many as 50 states in the USA have been classified as being at risk of potential disasters and long-term dangerous changes.

However, experts warn that adapting to climate change at the scale of entire coastlines and metropolitan areas will need more than floating houses, solid floors, waterproof plaster and walls, or improved weather warning systems. It may mean relocation of people or even cities. The Environment Agency has told the BBC that the UK is moving from a period of 'known extremes' of weather to one of 'unknown extremes'.[12] The floods of winter 2015 testify to that. There is also a growing school of thought that it is futile to try and prevent climate change and therefore the aim should be to mitigate its worse effects – an adaptive and autotelic effort rather than an aggressive one. An

130 The autotelic architect

example of an autotelic response to flooding would be the actions taken by the architect and Governor of the State of Paraná, Brazil, Jaime Lerner. In 1994 and 1998, Lerner was elected Governor of the State of Paraná, in which Curitiba lies. Instead of building levees to protect Curitiba from floodplains like wealthier cities such as New Orleans and Sacramento in the USA have chosen to do, he made them into water parks. New Orleans Dutch Dialogues Workshops looked at creative ways to bring wetland landscaping into the city itself, another concept to make space for water.

According to Hank Dittmar, a consultant who advises governments on cities and sustainability, the long-term challenge will be a

> core one for architects, planners and engineers over the coming decade ... Learning how to adapt, to build resilient communities and how to respond to multiple design objectives in the larger environment are huge challenges which our professional and educational systems are only beginning to contemplate.[13]

While richer nations might have the resources to deal with climate change, poorer nations are more likely to suffer. Internal and external migration will only increase in the wake of disasters, crop failures and the failure of local nation states to respond – thus needing an autotelic response from those in charge of their built environment. So naturally, architects and planners in the poorer countries have had to embrace more radical approaches to both climate change and urbanisation by encouraging the development of rapid public transport systems, embracing renewable sources of energy and denser mixed-use development, in India, Colombia, Brazil, Turkey and many other countries. Some 94.5 per cent of Uruguay's electricity now comes from renewables, and prices are lower than in the past relative to inflation. There are also fewer power cuts because a diverse energy mix means greater resilience to droughts. Many poor countries are able to take such action because their consumption economy is already low – we might call this austerity. These lessons and solutions are important lessons for richer nations as all nations will face the burden of scarcity sooner or later.

Many small British architectural practices and charities work in countries already afflicted by scarcity, extreme weather, war and terrorism. Some larger UK architectural and engineering practices also offer pro-bono work for such 'development work'. However, such

Figure 4.2 Rising sea levels in places like Venice threaten to destroy more than a thousand years of architectural heritage that connects the East and West. Rising sea levels are a direct consequence of thermal expansion caused by the warming of the oceans (since water expands as it warms) and the loss of land-based ice (such as glaciers) due to increased melting. Flood mitigation will need to involve thinking about strategic land use, individual building design and details as well as cooperation between nations

Source: author.

132　The autotelic architect

work, although very much in need, is limited because larger charities such as Oxfam who commission such work do not want to use architects who they view as a 'luxury'. So the only option so far has been for architects to open their own charities (as I and many other practices have done). Acknowledging the growing importance of an architectural response to climate change and the urban environment and what architects can do, RIBA hosted an international conference in June 2015 called 'Designing City Resilience' and an exhibition 'Creation from Catastrophe: How architecture rebuilds communities' in 2016. While such actions might have been unthinkable for RIBA to host even five years ago, the challenges brought by the scarcity of resources in an increasingly unequal and chaotic world mean that it is a timely recognition that such a negative situation also offers opportunities for architects and planners to affect the world in a positive way.

Autotelic architects are finding subversive ways of highlighting the clash of nature, buildings, urban regeneration and social and climate change through public projects. An example of this would be the 230-foot 'Sea Organ' in the city of Zadar, Croatia, created in 2005. The reconstruction of Zadar after World War II left a long concrete shoreline that was taken as a starting point for a 'Sea Organ', where wind and water from the Adriatic Sea are channelled in and out of holes that lead into chambers, creating mesmerising and haunting music. This was designed by a Croatian architect, Nikola Bašić. Since then it has become a popular lunch-spot for both visitors and locals. After this, Bašić created a LED light installation entitled Greeting to the Sun, designed to respond to the Sea Organ's installation. The circular floor installation consists of 300 multilayered glass plates encasing solar cells that absorb sunlight during the day and come alive at night, putting on a spectacular light show. In Taiwan, an abandoned shopping mall built in the 1980s in downtown Tainan has become an opportunity for the Dutch firm MVRDV's lagoon-inspired proposal that references Tainan's natural landscape and historic role as a marine and fishing industry hotspot.

Ageing and healthy cities

According to Fast Future, a consultancy firm that studies trends, many of today's 10 or 11 year olds will live to at least 120 and a sizeable proportion will keep working until they reach 100. With such long working lives, it predicts that workers will adopt a 'portfolio'

Figure 4.3 The Sea Organ and Greeting to the Sun by Nikola Bašić
Sources: Pieter Navis (top) and Zahgreb Tourist Agency (bottom).

134 The autotelic architect

approach to employment, meaning they could have as many as ten different, shorter careers, including 40 different jobs. Demographics in the UK are slowly confirming these predictions. The number of people over the age of 90 was more than half a million in 2015, according to the ONS. The Oxford Institute of Population Ageing predicts that most jobs as we know them will no longer exist when today's children reach 100. Robots will work alongside humans, making physically demanding tasks obsolete, while working patterns will be less regimented, instead fitting around lifestyles and family time.

The ageing population will mean a rethink of not just homes but also cities. The 'Silver Linings' report[14] highlighted the needs of our ageing population in cities. As we live longer, our buildings and homes have to be adaptive to be able to cater for a variety of needs, such as less mobility, diminishing eyesight or hearing, etc. Climate change with its extremes of temperatures will affect the elderly more. There are 11.4 million people aged 65 and over in the UK, according to the ONS. Charity Independent Age say that 36 per cent of them do not heat their homes adequately in winter because of worries about paying fuel bills, while 13 per cent have resorted to going to a library, a shopping centre or using public transport just to stay warm in winter. In France, the NOMADE Architectes Agency completed housing for the elderly in Concoret in the Loire region in 2013. The town now has the first 'BBC Effinergie' labelled accommodation facility for the elderly in France. Apart from providing residents with a stimulating social environment, it also is a high-performance, energy-efficient structure set within a salubrious rural environment of fields and forests.

By 2051, it is predicted that over two million people in the UK will have dementia and more care homes will need to be built that are adaptive to these complex needs of ageing. Designing for people with mental health problems, which is on the rise not just among the elderly but also in younger people, is another challenge for the autotelic architect. As 'care in the community' becomes more prevalent, instead of separate care homes, we will see more retrofitting of existing houses to cater for the demands of the less mobile, visually impaired or for those with dementia. This is a sector that needs a participative and collaborative approach, engaging with patients, artists and healthcare specialists. More enlightened examples of procurement of housing for ageing come from the continent, especially the Scandinavian countries and Japan (where people routinely live longer than other countries). In the Netherlands, De Rokade Groningen, by Arons en

The autotelic architect 135

Gelauff Architecten,[15] is conceived as a vertical city for 'younger seniors' within the Maartenshof continuing care facility. Instead of the sector's customary low-key architecture, this building announces itself with its high-rise facades punctuated by circular holes. This particular project that was completed in 2009 is also part of the 2003 'Intense City' to keep the city compact by increasing the building density of districts around the centre. Healthcare for the elderly and others in the Scandinavian countries has always been more advanced with the focus on not only eye-catching design but also on a restorative environment using low-energy and 'indoor climate' management.

The architecture of transience and smallness

If the architectural profession is considered a 'boutique' profession, then small buildings form the biggest commissions for the profession. Small buildings fascinate the general public too – many architectural journals hold competitions specifically for homes, while the wider press love to feature architect-designed homes and gardens. Popular TV shows such as 'The House that 100K Built', 'Dream Homes', 'Grand Designs', 'Changing Rooms', etc., have brought architectural design closer to the public than the Stirling Prize ceremony. 'Ask an Architect' at the Homes and Renovation Show, the 'Architect in the House' event from the charity Shelter and other annual events bring architects closer to potential clients. For the autotelic architect, presenting shows or taking part in exhibitions brings their talent to those looking for it. Pluralism and complexity, along with scarcity of resources, has brought forth the architecture of transience, with its pop-ups, sheds and shop fronts, and even Lego and model kits (Arckits[16]) designed by architects. It is a world where architects compete for small projects, as tiny as shop fronts[17] and beach huts, to demonstrate their skills and willingness to engage with a disinterested world.

Other examples of transient architecture that attract and provoke public interest in architecture are pop-ups and pavilions. One such project is the hugely popular annual Serpentine Gallery pavilion. Although the annual pavilion started with a well-known architect, Zaha Hadid, and has featured others such as Peter Zumthor, the later ones have been commissioned to younger and unknown architects, particularly from overseas. Pop-up shops, boutiques and restaurants can be found everywhere now. Due to their transient nature, these can be erected in places where formal architectural commissions cannot or will not happen, such as disused petrol stations, under bridges

Figure 4.4 'Care home' for the elderly, Orestad, Copenhagen, by JJW Arkitekter. This project uses colour and an emphasis on both private and communal outside spaces – rooftop garden, terraces, patios – to give the complex youthful boldness. Most visually compelling are the trapezoidal private balconies that protrude out from the apartments, permitting residents to engage with the wider world

Source: Lisa Als Klein.

Figure 4.5 Chilean architect Smiljan Radić designed the fourteenth Serpentine Pavilion in 2014, a semi-translucent, cylindrical structure that resembled a giant cocoon. He was 'discovered' by the director of the Serpentine Gallery while exhibiting at the Venice Biennale in 2010, where he exhibited a 14-tonne boulder with a little wooden nest in its hollow. According to Radić, his country supports a culture of making and experimentation, with 40 architecture schools in its capital, Santiago, alone

Source: author.

138 The autotelic architect

and in buildings marked for demolition or further work. Younger practices have made such work a staple of their business, and this has brought them further work. Pop-up architecture can be braver than the conventional, knowing that its very transient nature means that it has to shout loudly for the short time it is there. Furthermore, these cost little compared to conventional work and are therefore more likely to be 'commission-friendly'.

Construction kits for homes and offices are becoming increasingly popular as they offer a quick installation and usually require no planning permission. From tree houses to prefabricated houses, the idea is to offer kits that can be easily put together by the client. IKEA, the grand daddy of flatpacks, has also taken on this trend by commissioning a kit house designed by an architect, as has the Danish product designers Vipp, but sadly both remain prototypes and are too expensive. However, those with an autotelic nature have discovered another way. Tiit Sild, former city architect of Tartu, Estonia, set up a web-based architecture marketplace start-up offering prefabricated timber houses that are designed by architects. However, this is not done in the usual way. An annual competition is held to judge the best designs for prefab and then the winners get a percentage of the profit when their work is sold. In 2014, a wide range of countries successfully participated in the competition, with entries from 21 countries, including Taiwan, Australia and the USA.

Some architects have found work by not building anything but showing what is called 'fictional' or 'paper' architecture. This is a portfolio of unbuilt projects that demonstrate at least a theoretical approach to design (pretty much like that of a student portfolio) and invite the possibility of future work. While they can be also a source of publicity, they have been referred to as 'Zombie architecture'. That many new practices show such unbuilt work on their websites is a testimony to changing practice – that by simply showing an interest, it may be possible to get further work. However, this method has to be treated cautiously – built projects should always be in higher proportion, otherwise it displays inexperience. For those starting out, getting permission to showcase what new graduates might have done in previous employment is a good way to start building up a portfolio of projects.

Figure 4.6 Transferable technology in the form of quick sandbag construction as used in California for earthquake-proof construction by architect Nader Khalili has been transported to a school in West London by Julian Faulkner (not an architect) to soundproof against aircraft noise in a scheme funded by Heathrow Airport

Source: author.

Figure 4.7 Four renovated Jubilee line train carriages have become offices in the non-profit venture, Village Underground, in East London. These are used as workspaces. In the main Village Underground centre, renovated, turn-of-the-century warehouses are used for concerts and club nights to exhibitions, theatre, live art and other performances

Source: author.

Thinking bigger

On bigger commissions, while many improvements have been made to the procurement process for public buildings through campaigns from RIBA and architects (for example Project Compass), they remain essentially a tick box facility that gives quantitative weighting based upon previous experience. The UK's procurement system freezes out younger and smaller practices due to an 'increasingly bureaucratic' system. Many new British practices have been able to work on large schemes abroad, despite lack of experience, because they look for talent and ideas. One architect said in an interview: 'The number of hurdles you have to pass through to get a commission is daunting and the amount of design work you have to do is daunting, demoralising and very wasteful.'[18]

So at present, an enlightened client or a big competition win are the only hopes of a small or young practice that wants to change sectors or move to bigger projects. Exhibiting at international events may also be able to open doors – the Venice Biennale, for example, has been the stepping stone for bigger and higher-value commissions for many small practices.[19] An example of an enlightened client might be the Serpentine Gallery where many unknown practices from abroad have secured work – conversely, having a piece of work in London gives them global recognition. The Chilean practice Smiljan Radic, for example, who designed the Serpentine Gallery pavilion in 2014, was 'discovered' by the director of the gallery at the Venice Biennale in 2011.

Even so, public commissions such as schools and hospitals are a good choice for a smaller practice, such as Phase 2 of the government's Priority Schools Building Programme under the Education Funding Agency. Accommodation for university students is also popular and will remain so as students flood into cities with universities from other parts of the UK and abroad. Many practices have identified private housing – in particular student housing – as the 'hottest' sectors.[20] The 2015 winner of the Stirling Prize for a school building has certainly boosted the enthusiasm for designing educational buildings. The UK currently has just under 30,000 schools serving 9.75 million pupils. More primary schools need to be built – 150 new schools every year until 2021, so this will remain a 'hot sector' for a while.

Buddhism describes the 'four sufferings' of man that are universally common – birth, sickness, ageing and death. As these functions are now mainly institutionalised, increasingly healthcare facilities and hospices will be needed – and will continue to remain a good

Figure 4.8 Ludwig Guttmann Healthcare Centre, by Penoyre and Prasad Architects, was originally designed as part of the London 2012 Olympic Games at Stratford, East London. As part of the London Legacy Development Corporation, it is now used as a community healthcare centre. Healthcare design opportunities will always be there for designers

Source: author.

source of work for the architect. While clearly the Private Finance Initiative system for hospitals has resulted in poor-quality designs with the burden of huge repayments, with many NHS Trusts going under, smaller healthcare projects funded differently have been more successful. These include the LIFT projects and community healthcare facilities. Privately commissioned Maggie's Centres have also been good for architects, although some complain that only 'starchitects' benefit from these commissions. These centres are hospices for cancer patients co-founded by and named after the late Maggie Keswick Jencks, who died of cancer in 1995. One of these buildings in Hammersmith designed by Rogers Stirk Harbour+Partners in 2009 remains the only healthcare building to win the Stirling Prize. Getting healthcare commissions can be good for smaller practices, leading on to other work. Guy Greenfield, who was relatively unknown in 2001 when his Hammersmith Doctor's Surgery received a RIBA award, became a finalist for the Stirling Prize. Extensively published, that project led to further healthcare work. Just four years later, the practice completed its own seafront residential development.

The UK's Health and Social Care Act 2013 has been about the decentralisation of the management of the NHS. At present, perhaps as a precursor to the future, hospitals are being urged to have an 'overbuild development strategy' including building a combination of 6, 12 or 18 storeys of flats above NHS buildings, which may optimise use of precious land resources, especially in the cities. Bringing healthcare to those who need it, healthcare facilities and smaller hospitals set intimately within a community will become commonplace. The digitisation of healthcare will allow patients, especially the old and vulnerable, to be supported in their own homes or community settings, for example the 'Virtual Physiological Human' developed by Sheffield University in 2014. In future healthcare culture, 'conventional' medical clinics could be placed within gyms, spas and other practices. Architects working in the healthcare area may find themselves collaborating not only with specialists such as those in housing or education but also with clinicians and allied healthcare professionals. Governments and policy-makers are increasingly recognising that buildings, neighbourhoods, cities and place-making can be part of a wider 'healthcare culture' placed in the context of the built environment – including crime prevention, education, diet and exercise, and reducing the income gap and pollution.

Urbanisation and city planning

Rapid urbanisation has brought on unbearable densities – Manila, for example, has more than 42,000 persons per square kilometre. High urban density is not the prerogative of poor countries alone – fourth and fifth most dense places are in France (Levallois-Perret and Le Pré-Saint-Gervais, both suburbs of Paris). Historically, pre-industrial cities with high densities have been the wealthiest and most dynamic, innovative,[21] diverse and ecologically sustainable due to their compact nature. The relationship between urban density and sustainability embraces environmental, social and behavioural factors. In 2013, a RIBA research report, Cities for Health, found that people who use outdoor urban spaces are healthier.

Housing provision is one of the main issues in cities, especially in bigger ones such as London. UK think tank the Adam Smith Institute says that 2.5 million new homes could be built and would take up less than 0.5 per cent of the landmass of England, but only with a radical reform of our planning system.

There are other reasons to look at mass housing again – housing projects won one-quarter of the awards at the Stirling Prize, and the housing sector brings in one-third of architectural fees.[22] However, rather than the recent past's emphasis on detailing and structure such as those of the passivhaus and smart homes, macro-level factors such as overall siting, massing, speed of construction and use of scarce resources are becoming the guiding inspiration for housing design. For example, in Milan, Boeri Studio has designed tree-filled sky-scrapers, *Bosco Verticale*, which create their own micro-climate by producing humidity, absorbing CO_2, filtering dust, providing shade and reducing noise. After this award-winning scheme, they plan to build a similar one in Lausanne, Switzerland.

Debates about the siting of new housing continue – according to the think tank Adam Smith Institute, London's housing crisis could be solved by allowing the construction of one million new homes on 3.7 per cent of green belt land within walking distance of a railway station. The 2014 Wolfson Economics 'Garden Cities' competition organised by the Policy Exchange revealed that architects and planners were thinking deeply and laterally about siting, density and resources. The 2015 New London Architecture competition 'New Ideas for Housing' also brought up some radical new suggestions. It attracted over 200 entries from 16 countries around the world, from world-renowned architects, developers, consultants, local boroughs and even laypersons. The 100 shortlisted ideas included both practical

Figure 4.9 City-centre parks provide an oasis for humans and animals, clean the air and bring welcome relief from the business of urban life. This park is in central London. With 47 per cent green spaces with 13,000 wildlife, there has been a move to declare London as a national park

Source: author.

146   The autotelic architect

and more radical ideas and ranged from increasing self-building and co-housing, to building over infrastructure assets, infilling council estates, and densifying the suburbs. On the continent, architects and planners are coming up with innovative solutions to place community facilities within rising densities – with Germany, the Netherlands and Belgium being at the forefront. Bustling city centres are often safer, and community facilities are localised – and, importantly, allow citizens to engage.[23] Some key design solutions to emerge include hospitals that work like hotels with checking in and out facilities (Germany), healthcare provision within infill sites and monuments (Belgium) and urban zoning and water reuse (Singapore), while co-housing (Sweden) remains very popular. It is thought that new technologies such as 3D printing will play a major part in the provision of the 3 billion new homes needed by 2030. Over half of building firms surveyed globally[24] said they are committed to incorporating sustainability into their work. Research suggests that people living in green homes are happier and healthier, with respiratory illnesses such as asthma particularly reduced – proving that sustainable building design has benefits beyond just the environment.

Global expansion

By 2008, about 75 per cent of the buildings needed in Western Europe by 2020 were already constructed. More than 70 per cent of those buildings were constructed in the past 20 years. So naturally architects are now working on overseas projects. For example, the Middle East is now the biggest single market for London-based Zaha Hadid Architects, with the region accounting for 40 per cent of the firm's business. According to the UN, the world will be 60 per cent urbanised in 2030. Cities in Asia and South America, in particular, are expanding rapidly, with the majority of mega cities located there. However, both East and West have been at fault when it comes to the design of cities, according to Bernard Tschumi, the architect and planner whose father, Jean, was one of the founders of UIA. He says:

> I do think that architects … have completely failed in their mission to design the city of today or tomorrow. I think we are all responsible, I probably am, as much as my whole generation … At the moment they are mostly all alike, especially when we talk about the Middle East or China … In the cities of the 'historical West', London, Paris, Munich and so on, an incredible timidity has somehow replaced the extraordinary ideas and thinking processes that were taking place

throughout the 20th century: in the '20s, the '30s, the '40s, the '50s, the '60s, even including the '70s. I hope that we can call it a period of transition. As history has shown, when the work is too banal, irritation sets in, followed by critique, and then theory possibly comes back. This is my hope for the city of tomorrow.[25]

The global construction market is expected to grow by 85 per cent to $15.5 trillion worldwide by 2030, new research shows, with China, the USA and India leading the way and accounting for 57 per cent of all global growth. As 'emerging markets' will overtake 'developed markets' by 10 per cent in 2050, working globally offers new and established architectural practices exciting opportunities. As an engineer says, 'Enormous benefits await those who can adapt their thinking for global working' and describes how a 'constant revelation has been the way local construction teams, contractors and labour forces have been able to turn drawings into reality with less effort than we have found recently in the UK'.[26] And there is plenty of work available as newly wealthy nations declare their importance by building shiny totems of success. While large-scale cities are the prerogative of large practices, smaller projects are being taken on by smaller practices. Younger and smaller practices may find that working overseas enhances their reputation at home. Equally, after having success in the UK, practices may feel confident about working overseas. After winning the Stirling Prize in 2014, the director of Haworth Tompkins declared: 'We are ready to work internationally.'[27]

Poor nations have realised the economic benefits of having iconic buildings, i.e. 'the Bilbao effect', to demonstrate their progress, invite investment and attract tourists. It seems that new shopping malls, airports, hotels and office buildings are being designed by smaller practices every day in some part of the globe. Now plans have been unveiled to build Africa's tallest skyscraper in Casablanca, Morocco. It has been designed by Paris-based practice Valode & Pistre and, at 540m, will be more than double the continent's current tallest tower, the 223m Carlton Centre in Johannesburg, a city situated in a much wealthier country. According to the architect, the design of Al Noor Tower is derived from a 'wedding dress' and that the height of 540m is a reference to the 54 nations of Africa. But it adds that the new building will be more than a showpiece – it is a programme to increase employment and tourism and bring prosperity to the country, with a huge benefit for the population and the government. It is due to be completed in 2018. Whether such new iconic projects bring

148 The autotelic architect

peace and prosperity to a nation remains to be seen, but the reality is that the cities where these projects will be situated continue to be chaotically planned, with millions of their inhabitants at the mercy of the vagaries of climate change, internal strife and inequalities.

Looking at slums, a radical concept emerged from Medellin, in Colombia, where architect-designed facilities such as schools and library parks (which include day-care services, auditoriums and community rooms) have been placed in the slums of the city using the credo 'the most beautiful buildings for the poorest areas'. This novel idea from Mayor Sergio Fajardo was to bring in people and visitors from other parts of the city, thereby creating a sense of civic pride and dignity, and consequently reducing vandalism and crime. Fajardo is a mathematician-turned-politician who found that grass-roots action, combined with strict law and order, was the way to turn a city of crime into a tourist destination. So far Medellin has been an outstanding success because the Mayor started with the people first, commissioning buildings that benefited them rather than commissioning a building that might attract tourists alone. This concept has benefited the city and its citizens, architects and tourists widely.

As seen from the example of Medellin, solutions in the city emerge from focusing on a common goal and asking fundamental questions about society. A young Thai practice called Supermachine began the design process by asking a central question, 'How will people live in the near future?', and ended up with a community-use project called 'The Staircase' built by a multi-skilled crew. Fundamentally a vertical labyrinth, it encourages interaction, exercise and fun. Funded and supported by the project owner, Siam Cement Group, the biggest construction material manufacturer in Thailand, this project won the AR Emerging Architecture Award for 2015. Their final design looked into contemporary Thai culture with 'its banality and vibrancy while envisioning the future of community design'.[28] Such collaborative efforts also engender a sense of community, something that is fast disappearing in many urban centres. These kind of small interventions are much more effective than iconic structures that drain the country and fall into disrepair after the event (as happened in China and other places after the Olympic Games).[29]

Time and time again, it has been shown that architecture is a source of rejuvenation of society, including economic and cultural. So the 'Bilbao effect' is not a recent phenomenon. Take Japan, for instance. After the devastation of World War II, by 1968 Japan rose to become the world's second largest economy. Architecture was instrumental

Figure 4.10 The Staircase by Supermachine, Thailand. Young practices such as Supermachine are coming up in the new economies. This structure sits in a park near Bang Saen Beach, a coastal resort 60 miles east of the Thai capital. The concrete structure has been nicknamed 10 Cal Tower because a person apparently loses that many calories climbing to the top

Source: Supermachine.

150 The autotelic architect

in this process, which reached its climax at the Osaka Expo of 1970. This happened as architects re-examined their relationship with society against a background of environmental pollution, global political problems and the oil crisis, leading to the flowering of a distinctly Japanese style of architecture. Now the once-thriving 'motor city' of Detroit in the USA, which became a 'ghost city' after it lost its people and jobs to its suburbs or other states or nations, is using architecture to kick start its economy. With an unemployment rate of 15 per cent, the city was declared bankrupt in 2013. So now it is trying to reinvent itself as an 'entertainment city' with the opening of casinos, stadiums and a riverfront project. However, small-scale projects in the city such as urban gardens and agriculture, woodlands (Hantz Farms – where 15,000 trees were planted on 20 acres of vacant land) and the removal of 'urban blight' with the creation of new homes may be more effective than casinos in bringing the sense of community back as well as making the city more sustainable.

The UK's biggest tourist attraction, the 'London Eye' – a huge Ferris wheel on the South Bank of the Thames – was the brainchild of architects Julia Barfield and David Marks. At the time they proposed the scheme, the idea seemed almost a fantasy, but persistence and courage paved the way for its unique construction. Borrowing on the traditional fairground image, it was something that visitors could relate to immediately and it quickly became a popular landmark. Richard Rogers commented:

> The Eye has done for London what the Eiffel Tower did for Paris, which is to give it a symbol and to let people climb above the city and look back down on it. Not just specialists or rich people, but everybody. That's the beauty of it: it is public and accessible.[30]

The former Mayor of Bristol, George Ferguson, who has been a past President of RIBA and is an architect, has used his autotelic skills as a leader to make his city the 'Green Capital of Europe' and commissioned many innovative projects during his tenure, calling it his 'best job' yet.

Working with existing structures

There is always work available in the form of preservation of heritage buildings, almost anywhere in the world. Such specialised work takes time to learn, but there are special courses, such as those offered by the Society for the Protection of Ancient Buildings in the UK and

Figure 4.11 The London Eye was designed by a team led by architects David Marks and Julia Barfield. Finished in March 2000, it was first known as the Millennium Wheel or latterly as the 'London Eye' prefixed with its various corporate owners – British Airways, Merlin Entertainments, EDF Energy and presently the Coca-Cola London Eye. Eye-catching design is always desired by larger corporations

Source: author.

152 The autotelic architect

many others offered at universities and further education colleges. RIBA also has a specialist register for those architects working in conservation, and there is also the Architects Accredited in Building Conservation scheme to reassure potential clients. In 2013, companies based in listed buildings contributed £47 million (I assume this precludes our Parliament building, which will cost £3.5 billion to upgrade over 32 years!) and produced a heritage premium of over £13,000 per occupying business per year compared to the average. The heritage-based tourist economy added £14 billion to GDP in 2013. Work on listed buildings basically consists of two types: conservation and repair; and adaptation. For the autotelic architect, conversions of existing buildings, including those that are listed, offers a growing source of work. But this is reuse and conversion with a twist. For example, the 2013 Stirling Prize winner, the twelfth-century ruins of Astley Castle in Warwickshire, although Grade II* listed, was subtly and skilfully adapted to become a Landmark Trust guesthouse for eight people.

Responding to the needs of conservation while also reusing all or part of the building can be carbon friendly and aspirational. Not using an architect in such projects can be seriously risky. Many other reuse projects have taken refurbishment on to a more sophisticated scale than just restoration. An office conversion of a set of buildings built between 1910 and 1930 incorporates a cycle ramp, bar, basketball court, 5m-long kitchen table and library. This project by RHE Architects in Shoreditch, London, engages the desire for new ways of travelling and working. Part of Preston Bus Station (a Brutalist structure) is to be converted into a youth centre, under a scheme proposed by the council and Preston Youth Zone, while continuing to be used as a bus station. Worldwide, conservation and the reuse of existing buildings and structures are also on the rise. The highly successful and much-imitated High Line project in New York is situated on an elevated section of a disused New York Central Railroad spur called the West Side Line. Itself inspired by the 3-mile (4.8-kilometre) *Promenade Plantée* (tree-lined walkway), a similar project in Paris completed in 1993, the High Line has become an urban oasis and an elevated garden. In Budapest's Buda Castle, the regeneration of the 'castle garden bazaar' by the architect Mikl.s Ybl, abandoned since the 1980s, was opened in 2014 as a new 'cultural and entertainment centre'.

Another sadly neglected area but a great source of work could be the retrofit of existing buildings. To simply demolish disused buildings is

Figure 4.12 UAL campus for Central Saint Martins, inside the nineteenth-century Grade II-listed granary building and transit sheds at King's Cross Goods Yard, London. The £200 million new University of the Arts London campus unites all its activities under one roof for the first time for the institution. The surrounding landscape of 67 acres containing derelict industrial buildings is being transformed as part of Europe's largest urban regeneration project

Source: author.

Figure 4.13 High Line Project by Diller Scofidio+Renfro, New York. Though a much humbler project than iconic buildings, since 2009 this urban park has brought about the revitalisation of nearby areas with a museum and 30 other real-estate developments in the neighbourhoods that lie along the line. Needless to say, it has brought worldwide fame and work to the architects

Source: Soumya Dharmavaran.

The autotelic architect   155

a great waste of resources – unfortunately, as the BBC2 documentary series called 'Demolition: The Wrecking Crew' showed in May 2015, this is now a billion pound industry, and therefore a lucrative market for building contractors and for those who cannot be bothered to think about the reuse of buildings. In the UK, the motivations for the radical energy demand reduction that can be achieved by retrofit are many. As well as climate change, security of supply has become an issue now that the country is increasingly reliant on fuel imports with the attendant risks of interrupted supply and fluctuations in price. (After the closure of the coal mines, most of the UK's coal comes from abroad, although ironically many of the coal-fired stations sit on coal seams.) Energy from renewable sources, such as wind farms, produce only around 10 per cent of the UK's needs.[31] There exists a real threat to power cuts from 2015 onwards, even in the UK, necessitating the need to lower energy from buildings. Some 51 per cent of architects, engineers, contractors, owners and consultants participating in a study carried out in 62 countries in 2012 anticipated that more than 60 per cent of their work will be green by 2015, up from 28 per cent previously. And the growth of green construction is not limited to one geographic region or economic state – it is spreading throughout the global construction marketplace. In order to meet our energy targets, 3.5 million non-domestic and 26 million residential buildings have to be retrofitted.[32]

The roll-out of street-by-street retrofit, at a scale that will be necessary to meet these challenges, will be a difficult task. Retrofit is complicated with the logistical problems involved with decanting occupants, and retrofit's general disruption is exacerbated by the huge variety of dwelling types, including those in conservation areas. Just like now there is a national discussion about flood defences and prioritising of human lives over wildlife, in the future such discussions may extend to heritage compared with ecological impact. Some of the most expensive properties in London[33] are some of the worst-performing from an energy point of view.[34] Both retrofit and design for a sustainable future require innovative ideas to prioritise the competing demands, and compromises, required for our collective future. At present, 57 per cent of EU architects are working on refurbishment projects, which include retrofit, and this market is bound to grow.

A project by the architects of the London Eye, David Marks and Julia Barfield, to retrofit their own home that lies in a conservation area of South London has given impressive results after two years of post-occupancy monitoring – it averages only 30kg of CO_2/sq m per year. Julia Barfield says:

Figure 4.14 A retrofit housing project using insulation made from discarded clothes. Designed by Jean-Luc Collet, architect for the Pas-de-Calais habitat housing association within the EU Interreg Project IFORE (Innovation for Renewal, www.ifore.eu)

Source: Mike McEvoy.

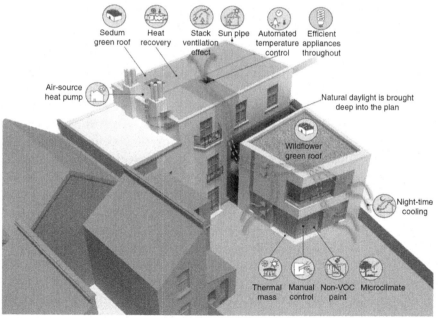

Figure 4.15 A retrofit of a home in a conservation area by Marks Barfield Architects

Sources: Timothy Soar; Marks Barfield.

158 The autotelic architect

It's relatively simple to build new housing to high environmental standards. The [real] challenge is the existing housing stock. Even harder is to achieve this in a conservation area. Since London has almost half of the UK's estimated dwellings in conservation areas, it is imperative to find ways to square this circle.[35]

Dr Mike McEvoy, who has worked on a large scheme for retrofitting homes in Kent, says:

Retrofit is assumed to be glorified maintenance, a technological issue free of value judgements – outside of the sophisticated debate about architecture. But it is a complex and technically challenging operation dependent upon performance and how it is measured, not just a concern for the extended life of buildings.[36]

Creative collaborations

As mentioned before, the future generation are more likely to work in a loose collaborative among themselves rather than for a power above. Participation encourages a collaborative process that can be more complex and slow but enriches the end product, which has more significance to the users. Through participation, the participants can also influence decision-making for future projects and strengthen democratic processes. Multidisciplinary built environment think tank The Edge, established in 1995, even called its year-long Commission of Inquiry on the Future of Professionalism in the UK's design and construction industries 'Collaboration for Change', published in May 2015.[37] In a RIBA study about the future of architects, expanded modes of practice offering a broader range of services would seem to be a key trend for the future. Many architects in the study felt restricted by the term 'architect' and instead preferred to be known as 'spatial agencies' or 'design houses'. In this group would come other creative workers such as set designers and installation and fine artists. The Internet has made the process of collaboration and sharing easier and on a scale not seen before. The autotelic nature of collaborator arising from an internal driver is very different to the nature of 'architect as the supreme leader', as seen in the past.

The days when Frank Lloyd Wright or Charles Rennie Mackintosh would not only design the building, but also the cutlery to be used there, have long gone – the architect is more likely to collaborate at the micro level with people who specialise in their crafts. Instead of

Figure 4.16 Another pop-up! TREExOFFICE in Hoxton Square, London, by architecture studio Tate Harmer. Built by Atom Build, in collaboration with artist Natalie Jeremijenko and Shuster+Moseley, installation artists and 'philosophers'. Design team included structural engineers Price and Myers and briefing architects Gensler

Source: author.

being the artist, the architect is more likely to commission an artist. This is a win–win situation. In an office project, architects EPR, for example, commissioned artist Kate Malone to create hand-glazed tiles to face the building in order to create an 'attention-grabbing' facade. According to the architects:

> Architects and artists actually come from quite different disciplines, so the success of your product depends on the dialogue with each other ... [This project] has been a true collaboration between architecture, art and artisan manufacturing and the relationship between us has been exceptional.[38]

The artist says: 'I would like to see architects using the brilliant crafts talent we have in this country a lot more – it would definitely benefit the built environment and the communities that occupy it.'[39] One can see that there has been a shift in the relationship as well, one where the architects are increasingly commissioning artists not only to make their buildings beautiful but also adding a social purpose to it. Many healthcare buildings also put a small part of their budgets towards art installations.

Collaboration also happens between architects and other professionals and artists as an organisational structure. Many architectural practices like to refer to themselves as 'design collaboratives'. They include within their practice graphic designers, artists, photographers, sculptors and other creatives. London-based Muf and Japanese community architects, studio-L, based in Tohoku are examples of such collectives who not only work collectively but also participatively within the community. Studio-L works by making friends first and finding a core group of people who are allocated specific tasks – such groups are called 'constellations'. These core people attract further people to help them to do the work. Each project takes an average of three years to complete. Work is 'people-scaled', i.e. what can be done with ten people, what can be done with 100 people, etc. Having such a diverse group of professionals and creatives make the practice innovative, self-sufficient and self-sustaining (by having diverse sources of income). Even bigger practices such as Foster + Partners are not averse to collaboration with such smaller practices. In 2014, Norman Foster visited the offices of Mexico-based FR-EE in New York. From that meeting and a promise of future collaboration began an association when FR-EE won a competition to design a much larger project, the Mexico City airport, a typology in which Foster +

The autotelic architect 161

Partners were well versed.[40] According to FR-EE, their 'Airport of the Future' is designed with inspiration from Mexico's history but looks to the future by being 'the most sustainable airport in the world, the first with the LEED certification'.[41]

Other forms of collaboration that are going to be increasingly significant to the small practice are collaborations with clients. Many prospective clients decide to build or extend their own houses either due to fears about the architect's fees or because they want to have control over the process. But they fail to recognise the architect's skills and, as many TV programmes show, run into serious problems, including what they wanted to avoid in the first place – rising costs and complications. On the other hand, we have many successes, most notably the lawyer who built his own 'hi-tech' house, the 'Tree House', in South London. For financial reasons, the client opted to go ahead with the build without the architect, who was a friend. Armed with a set of technical drawings and nothing more than a 'gentleman's agreement' with the subcontractors, the house was built to critical acclaim. But the real story is that of the architect whose core design concept was carried through to the end – otherwise architecturally it could have been a 'dog's dinner'.[42] In 2013–2014, half of new projects won by architects was the result of a direct approach from the client. The biggest beneficiaries of this were the micro-practices of whose direct commission made up more than 60 per cent, while the medium-sized firms got 45 per cent of their work this way.[43]

The other collaborations use virtual platforms. They could be in the form of idea sharing and newsletters for artists, furniture and jewellery designers and other crafts, and include news magazines or e-zines such as 'Design Boom' (originating from Italy), 'Dezeen' (originating from the UK) or 'Architecture in Development' (based in the Netherlands). Other platforms may be more about working together rather than just information sharing. jovoto, for example, is a Berlin-based collaborative founded in 2007 that operates internationally with more than 80,000 creative professionals, including architects. By using what they call 'crowdstorming' or large-scale virtual brainstorming and creative conversations, they solve problems by turning the creative challenge itself into a media event. To date, Jovoto has worked with more than 100,000 creative talents and successfully organised more than 250 challenges for large brands. They say:

> We believe that solving today's complex problems requires interdisciplinary talent, deeper insights and broader inspiration.

162   The autotelic architect

Imagine how powerful a creative process can get, fuelled by thousands of architects, product designers, inventors and artists, all thinking about the same problem at the same time?[44]

Becoming unreasonably autotelic

'The reasonable man adapts himself to the world. The unreasonable one persists in trying to adapt the world to himself. Therefore all progress depends on the unreasonable man.'[45] On his website, Richard Branson uses this quote from G.B. Shaw to urge us to become more 'unreasonable'. He says: 'Every entrepreneur should strive to be unreasonable, to push their business to become a force for good, and create more innovation, more change and more progress.'[46] Unlike G.B. Shaw's day, being unreasonable is not a failure of character but a positive sign. Alexa Clay, who travelled the world talking to computer hackers, gang leaders and Amish camel farmers, has written a book called *The Misfit Economy*[47] about corporate rebels who refuse to conform. Therefore, there is no time like the present for being an autotelic architect. An important aspect of working in an autotelic manner would be acceptance and going with the flow, like surfing the big waves that society throws up from time to time. This is not new – it just appears to be new. Hopefully this chapter illustrates that architecture is alive and kicking. It is the flailing practice and education of architects that we must revive. The three key qualities of an autotelic architect are flexibility, adaptability and collaboration, as seen from the previous discussion and examples. According to the proponents of chaos theory, Silvio Funtowicz and Jerry Ravetz, the future belongs to professionals 'who specialize in uncertainties and value choices in their work. For them, each case is unique. [They] confront issues where facts are uncertain, values in dispute, stakes high and decisions urgent.'[48]

Do we have to fear the future? Let's take automation and artificial intelligence. According to Deloitte, automation has replaced 800,000 jobs in the past 15 years – mainly the 'nasty and boring ones'.[49] Already we have automated switchboards, email sorting, driverless cars and trains, and even automated farming – automation of our lives is increasing exponentially. As construction work is increasingly automated using drones and 3D printers, mid-to-low-skill construction jobs are most at risk. But jobs that require high levels of creativity, empathy and problem-solving will be safe because artificial intelligence cannot match these human traits, as has been

The autotelic architect 163

said: 'To compare complex, unpredictable, emergent biological and social systems to the very logical, deterministic world of computer software is at best a dramatic oversimplification.'[50] According to research carried out by Erik Brynjolfsson and Andrew McAfee, creative industries are one of the likeliest industries to succeed in the age of artificial intelligence and automation.[51] According to an online interactive tool from the BBC, architects have only a 2 per cent chance of their work being taken over by automation. Roles requiring employees to think on their feet and come up with creative and original ideas, for example designers or engineers, hold a significant advantage in the face of automation.

So most architects' creative work appears to be safeguarded for the future. However, in RIBA's 'Client and architect: Developing the essential relationship' report, it has been claimed that architects who can design a building all the way from concept to delivery are such a rare breed that clients claim they are often forced to replace the original practice after planning. The report found clients regard the profession as falling into two broad and separate categories: the concept architect and the technical architect. According to the round table panellists, the very same creative flair that makes a good concept architect 'is an unacceptable risk during technical delivery'.[52] While I accept that there are many types of architects – those who are good at creative tasks while others are more technically able – it would also be good to have a third type – an architect who can do it all the way through. The other alternative is where the architects design and other co-professionals deliver (like in Design and Build) – which is happening anyway. So this is not really a divisive issue, assuming that different types of architects can work well with each other and with their co-professionals.

For an autotelic architect, the struggle to find work itself can become a space for experimentation and reflection – and networking, as it did for John Soane. According to architects Sheila O'Donnell and John Tuomey, their practice accumulated ideas from a variety of sources, including art and everyday objects such as a simple folding chair, and they fed this into their work. The time when the practice struggled to find work during its early years gave them the chance to think about and develop their approach to architecture. Liz Diller from the US firm Diller Scofidio+Renfro started the practice during the recession when there were very few architectural commissions. They bided their time, and 'the early years gave them an opportunity to take a critical stand and challenge what architecture is and

164   The autotelic architect

how it can interact with other cultural disciplines'.[53] Like O'Donnell, Liz Diller says that their early work was also ephemeral. There were many guerrilla installations on stolen or borrowed sites. Not having clients or funding, they were on borrowed money for many years until they slowly began getting recognition.

Technology is advancing rapidly, using many of the things we already use or see in daily life. For example, 3D goggles used in the cinema are being used by architects to create better designs, so that flaws not spotted in plans can be seen and photo-realistic renderings can be made quickly. Plans and images can be sent to the client's smartphone and even suggest changes. Virtual reality is changing the way designers work. Apart from the ability to work anywhere, the digitisation of work has made other kinds of compatibility possible between industries. The Internet is shaking up established industries, and the digital revolution is pulling things along – Airbnb being an example that has shaken up the hotel industry. We need to think about how to capture the advantages offered by these 'disruptive' technologies. For example, how could architects take advantage of the Airbnb revolution as interior designers are (John Lewis is even offering courses for people to do up their homes for Airbnb)? Could they persuade Airbnb entrepreneurs to use architects to spruce up their apartments with aspirational marketing such as 'architect-designed' apartments, like the way developers are doing?

On the other hand, the roles of RIBA and the ARB in the future of architecture must be questioned and reinvented, or otherwise they will become irrelevant to the 'digital nomads' of tomorrow. RIBA must become a place of security, knowledge and innovation that architects can look up to. It must campaign strongly for the survival of the architectural profession. While RIBA continues to do good things for the architect, it is still very much internally focused. It must start looking outside in, take the debate about architecture outside, engage meaningfully with the public, and campaign with the government and other policy-makers.

The other great social change that will influence the practice of architecture is the movement towards decentralisation, devolution and autonomy. Autonomy has also been a reason why digital technologies have become so popular. People want to be seen as individuals capable of doing things themselves, not being led by anyone. They like to work as a 'community of collaborators'. Organisations and institutions are no longer seen as powerful bodies but as old world, stuck in a time warp. Generation Z, the post-Millennials, are globally aware with no particular allegiance to anyone, whether an organisation or a practice. On the other hand, they are collaborative (as we have seen) and rely on technology for work and entertainment. They value experience more than knowledge and accumulation of wealth, freedom more than security and authenticity more than loyalty. To make architecture relevant for future architects, we need a vastly different way of education and practice – the movement has already started. This is the collaborative world, which engages with society, not turning away from it. Collaborations with our co-professionals, scientists and economists will also become important for sharing knowledge and creating effective designs to combat the vast problems that affect the planet, as discussed before. Foster + Partners and other large practices already work this way, but this way of working will also become the norm for small practices and even sole practitioners. James Dyson, virtuoso inventor and industrial designer, recommends that designers must collaborate with scientists and engineers.

Decentralisation and autonomy along with societal changes also mean that, if we don't do anything, the architect's traditional domain can be taken on by others. The meaning of the word 'designer' now is loose, multifaceted and all-embracing. Developers have also been doing it anyway, as we see in mass housing and now with other projects such as the Wunderland Kalkar in Germany – an unused power station that was saved from demolition by the Dutch entrepreneur Hennie van der Most, who purchased the site for a rumoured price of US$3 million. It has been repurposed into a tourist attraction that gets more than 600,000 visitors per year. No architect was reportedly involved in this project. Yves Béhar calls himself a designer, entrepreneur and 'sustainability advocate'. Now he has designed his own temporary exhibition pavilion made of timber, corrugated plastic and standard plywood on Miami Beach to showcase his products.

But entrepreneurial action from ordinary people is also not uncommon, as the numerous co-housing projects from the Scandinavian countries show. But now people also seem to be taking charge of their mortality, as a retirement co-housing project built in 2004 shows. The 'Herfra til Evigheden',[54] meaning 'From Here to Eternity' (from the 1953 film of the same name), is a co-housing scheme in Roskilde, Denmark. Some of the people are still working and some are retired but, led by the founding couple, all have taken part in every stage of the project: finding and buying the land; getting a loan; selecting consultants; and networking to find future co-residents. Acting as

Figure 4.17 Wunderland Kalkar is an amusement park near Düsseldorf, Germany. It is a theme park that calls itself the 'best hotel, party centre and family park in Germany'. It is centred around an unused nuclear power plant. Construction was started in 1972 but after the Chernobyl disaster in 1986, by 1991 the project was officially cancelled. Instead of demolishing it, many parts of the plant have been integrated into the park and its attractions, including the cooling tower, which features a swing ride and a climbing wall

Source: Wunderland Kalkar.

developer, client and occupier, the residents have been able to oversee the design and construction, and to sponsor variations between dwellings to complete the project. The lessons here are that if architects don't do it, someone else will.

At present, no one will notice if architects go on strike but, given the paucity of work, we might as well be on strike. The campaign to improve the status of architects must include ways to increase the fees paid to architects – this action alone will ensure that architecture as a profession survives and architecture students thrive. On the other hand, architects must learn to run their businesses properly. The Building Futures research indicates that small, specialised practices and bigger global consultancies and starchitects will become more prominent, while the mid-range practice with 25–30 people will decrease. This is already happening, and yet neither RIBA nor the practices themselves are reacting in an autotelic or even pro-active manner. In the same way, architectural schools must also change or even they will disappear, swallowed up by financial problems and a reduction in student numbers and demand. Highly respected schools of architecture have been threatened with closure but, thankfully, have been saved by campaigns by students, alumni and staff. However, nothing is secure, so we must continue to support them.

It is easy to predict the future from the wisdom of hindsight. At present, we do not know what will be happening to the planet in even five years' time, given the alarming predictions about climate change, rising population and global terrorism and crime. But we can try to pinpoint where architects might be now in among the innovators and leaders. Over 50 years ago, Everett Rogers, a professor of rural sociology, popularised the theory of 'Diffusion' in his book *Diffusion of Innovations*.[55] Rogers proposed that innovation spreads through the 'adopters', who could come from one of five types: innovators; early adopters; early majority; late majority; and laggards. Within the rate of adoption, there is a point at which an innovation reaches critical mass. Rogers showed that if these parameters were to be placed on a graph, they would form a slanting S-curve. Where do architects stand in this S-curve? Given that they are not a homogeneous mass and given the economic necessity to be extremely cautious, it is likely that most architects fall in the middle of the S. While uncertainty makes businesses, especially the small ones, keep their head down to concentrate on everyday work, they must be able to learn and adapt faster than the rate of change in their markets. Resilience is another characteristic of the autotelic architect, just as it is for the learner. The best kind of resilience, according to the psychotherapist Antonia Macaro, is to 'include acting to change things in the world as well as one's response to them. So even more important than resilience is the wisdom to know which kind of change is more relevant to us now.'[56]

Young Architect of the Year Awards are given to architects under 40 years – middle age for most and dinosaur-like compared to the ages of pop stars. Most architects in the EU reach their prime between the ages of 40 and 44, according to an ACE survey.[57] Like fine wine, we may be a late maturing profession, but age should not be a limiting factor in success. By 2030, there will be more of us above the age of 50 than below. We should celebrate talent wherever and whenever it appears. I cannot agree with a warning in *Architectural Review*: 'Numerous architects displaying early talent have failed to flower into full maturity as designers, in part because of the pressures that follow premature recognition.'[58] Bizarrely, this comment appears in the same issue that celebrated the wins of 'emerging new talent' of many young architects around the world. The sort of pressure that the writer describes is part of a young pop star's life, not a middle-aged architect's (I have yet to see inches of gossip columns in tabloids devoted to the private life or the dress worn by an architect). It is unnatural to expect someone to keep producing gems all throughout their working life – there will be some dud ones too. One exception was probably Frank Lloyd Wright, who reinvented his approach to design and aesthetics continuously, starting from his early 20s to his death at the age of 92 – an equivalent of the pop star Madonna in the world of architecture.

A belief that things will go on as they have is not a rational belief. Things will continue to change – there is no utopian vision but only the reality of change. However, our belief in the good things that architecture and architects bring to the world must overcome our despondency and dependency on external validation. As long as there are human beings on this planet, architecture will survive – of course, there has been, until now, more than 10,000 years of architecture but less than 200 years of architects. So I finish with another iteration of Gombrich's words I started with:

There really is no such thing as an architecture. There are only architects.[59]

Notes

1 http://newint.org/features/2015/12/01/alternatives-to-growth (accessed December 2015).
2 Capra (1982, p. 7).
3 Ibid.
4 A Buddhist phrase indicating that a negative can turn into a positive.
5 Toynbee (1997).
6 'Today Programme', BBC Radio 4, 2 January 2016.
7 A zero-carbon home must generate all its energy, including energy for heating, hot water, lighting and appliances, without adding carbon dioxide to the atmosphere. Depending on need, surplus energy can be exported and energy deficits can be met by importing energy, and the CO_2 emitted by burning biomass must be compensated for by exporting zero-carbon electricity to replace grid electricity. Taking these factors into account, the net amount of emissions must be zero over the space of a year.
8 www.treehugger.com/sustainable-product-design/buildings-account-for-half-of-all-co2-emissions.html (accessed September 2014).
9 www.wri.org/blog/2014/11/6-graphs-explain-world's-top-10-emitter (accessed November 2015).
10 www.theguardian.com/environment/2015/nov/09/worlds-climate-about-to-enter-uncharted-territory-as-it-passes-1c-of-warming (accessed November 2015).
11 Erika Spanger-Siegfried, the Union of Concerned Scientists' Climate and Energy Program. www.bbc.co.uk/news/world-us-canada-34872956 (accessed November 2015).
12 www.bbc.co.uk/news/uk-35188146 (accessed December 2015).
13 www.bdonline.co.uk/comment/opinion/climate-change-will-force-us-to-think-much-bigger-than-floating-houses/5078717.article (accessed November 2015).
14 'Silver linings: The active third age and the city', RIBA, 2013.
15 www.archdaily.com/1785/de-rokade-arons-en-gelauff-architecten (accessed November 2015).
16 'Arckits' was created by Irish architect Damien Murtagh. It is a modelling kit that provides the doors, walls, supports and roof tiles to create scale-model houses. Launched at Grand Designs 2014, the popularity of the kits has now spread to students of architecture, hobbyists, children and self-builders. It is now sold online and at Harrods as 'posh Lego'.
17 'Now in its sixth year, the RIBA Regent Street Windows Project pairs exceptional RIBA architects with flagship retailers to create engaging architectural installations in their shop windows.' www.architecture.com/RIBA/Contactus/OurUKoffices/London/regentstreet.aspx (accessed October 2015).
18 www.bdonline.co.uk/stirling-prize-winner-hits-out-at-uk-procurement/5071603.article (accessed October 2014).
19 www.dezeen.com/2014/12/04/selgascano-key-projects-serpentine-gallery-pavilion-2015 (accessed November 2015).

170 The autotelic architect

20 www.bdonline.co.uk/5071597.article?origin=BDdaily (accessed October 2014).
21 http://news.mit.edu/2013/why-innovation-thrives-in-cities-0604 (accessed November 2015).
22 www.bdonline.co.uk/5081692.article?origin=BDdaily (accessed May 2016).
23 www.theguardian.com/housing-network/2014/jul/29/cities-density-building (accessed November 2015).
24 62 countries were surveyed in the McGraw Hill Smart Market Report. www.worldgbc.org/files/8613/6295/6420/World_Green_Building_Trends_SmartMarket_Report_2013.pdf (accessed November 2015).
25 www.architectural-review.com/old/film/the-ar-interviews/interview-with-bernard-tschumi/8669431.fullarticle (accessed March 2016).
26 'Expand your mind', *RIBAJ*, November 2009, p. 20.
27 www.bdonline.co.uk/stirling-prize-winner-hits-out-at-uk-procurement/5071603.article (accessed October 2014).
28 www.architectural-review.com/buildings/reinventing-the-playground-supermachine-studios-10-cal-tower-in-thailand/8692372.fullarticle (accessed November 2015).
29 www.today.com/news/what-happens-olympic-venues-after-torch-goes-out-2D12152101 (accessed December 2015).
30 Rogers (2007).
31 'Power to the People', BBC4 series, 17 November 2015. The series went behind the scenes at energy company SSE, including one of Britain's biggest – and oldest – power stations, Ferrybridge C in Yorkshire.
32 'Shaping up for retrofit', *RIBAJ*, November 2014, p. 41.
33 www.theguardian.com/business/2014/may/19/savills-warns-uk-housing-crisis-shortage-new-homes (accessed June 2014).
34 Mike McEvoy, personal communication, November 2015 – 80 per cent of Camden Council's social housing stock is within conservation areas, a lot of it very difficult to retrofit economically.
35 'Instruments of change', *RIBAJ*, July 2013, p. 62.
36 Personal communication.
37 www.edgedebate.com/wp-content/uploads/2015/05/150415_collaboration forchange_book.pdf (accessed September 2014).
38 'Where art and architecture combine', *Architects Datafile*, July 2015, p. 29.
39 Ibid.
40 www.designboom.com/architecture/mexico-citys-new-airport-an-interview-with-fernando-romero-09-09-2014/?utm_campaign=monthly&utm_medium=e-mail&utm_source=subscribers (accessed November 2014).
41 www.fr-ee.org/project/5/New+Mexico+City+International+Airport (accessed September 2015).
42 'Products in practice', *RIBAJ*, March/April 2015, p. 16.
43 'Investment strategy', *RIBAJ*, February 2014, p. 46.
44 www.jovoto.com (accessed November 2015).
45 G.B. Shaw from the play *Man and Superman*, 1903.

The autotelic architect 171

46 www.virgin.com/richard-branson/the-unreasonable-man (accessed July 2015).
47 Clay (2015).
48 Sardar (2008, pp. 156–7).
49 BBC Panorama, 14 September 2015.
50 http://theurbantechnologist.com/2014/09/07/11-reasons-computers-cant-understand-or-solve-our-problems-without-human-judgement (accessed November 2015).
51 www.bbc.co.uk/news/technology-34175290 (accessed September 2015).
52 www.building.co.uk/clients-forced-to-replace-concept-architects-because-they-lose-interest/5077324.article (accessed September 2015).
53 www.designboom.com/architecture/liz-diller-interview-ds-r-11-27-2014 (accessed December 2014).
54 http://designobserver.com/feature/new-visions-of-home/14058 (accessed November 2015).
55 Rogers (1962).
56 www.ft.com/cms/s/0/3d9f4b4e-53e6-11e4-8285-00144feab7de.html#axzz42sNJJP7F (accessed November 2014).
57 www.ace-cae.eu/fileadmin/New_Upload/7._Publications/Sector_Study/2014/EN/2014_EN_FULL.pdf (accessed July 2015).
58 'Can early acclaim for an architect be a handicap – even the kiss of death?', *Architectural Review*, December 2015. Rather strangely, Enric Miralles, the Spanish architect who actually died prematurely at the age of 45, has also been used as an example for that quote.
59 Gombrich (1984, p. 4).

Bibliography

Aswan, Nishat, Schneider, Tatjana and Till, Jeremy, *Spatial Agency: Other Ways of Doing Architecture*, London: Routledge, 2011.

Aurelius, Marcus, *Meditations*, translated by Maxwell Staniforth, London: Penguin Classics, 2004.

Ayers, Andrew, *The Architecture of Paris: An Architectural Guide*, Paris: Edition Axel Menges, 2003.

Baldwin, J.M., *Dictionary of Philosophy and Psychology*, I 96/1, London: Macmillan, 1901.

Ballantyne, Andrew, *Architecture (Brief Insights)*, Oxford: Sterling, 2010.

Bayley, Stephen and Mavity, Roger, *Life's a Pitch: How to be Businesslike with Your Emotional Life and Emotional with Your Business Life*, London: Bantam Press, 2007.

Braungart, M. and McDonough, W., *Cradle to Cradle*, London: Vintage, 2009.

Bunch, Bryan and Hellemans, Alexander, *The Timetables of Technology: The Chronology of the Most Important People and Events in the History of Technology*, New York: Touchstone Books, 1994.

Capra, F., *The Turning of the Tide*, London: Wildwood, 1982.

Cartledge, Sarah, *The Guide to Global Opportunities*, London: Inspire Publishing on behalf of RIBA, 2014.

Chappell, David and Dunn, Michael, *The Architect in Practice*, Oxford: Wiley, 2016.

Cialdini, Robert B., *Influence: The Psychology of Persuasion.* New York: HarperBusiness. Revised edition, 2007.

Clark, Kenneth, *Civilisation: A Personal View*, London: The Folio Society, 1999.

Clay, Alexa, *The Misfit Economy*, New York: Simon & Schuster, 2015.

Crinson, Mark and Lubbock, Jules, *Architecture, Art or Profession? Three Hundred Years of Architectural Education in Britain*, Manchester: Manchester University Press, 1994.

Csikszentmihalyi, M., *Finding Flow: The Psychology of Engagement with Everyday Life*, New York: Basic Books, 1997.

Csikszentmihalyi, M., Rathunde, K. and Whalen, S., *Talented Teenagers: The Roots of Success and Failure*, New York: Cambridge University Press, 1993.

de Botton, Alain, *The Pleasures and Sorrows of Work*, London: Penguin Books, 2010.

Dobson, Adrian, *21 Things You Won't Learn in Architecture School*, London: RIBA Publishing, 2014.

174 Bibliography

Dolan, P., Hallsworth, M., Halpern, D., King, D. and Vlaev, I., *Mindspace: Influencing Behaviour Through Public Policy*, London: Cabinet Office and Institute for Government, March 2010.

Fraser, Murray, *Design Research in Architecture: An Overview*, Bartlett School of Architecture, UCL, Aldershot: Ashgate, 2013.

Fritjof, Capra, *The Turning Point*, London: Wildwood House, 1982.

Gombrich, E.H., *The Story of Art*, Oxford: Phaidon, 1984.

Handy, Charles, *Understanding Organisations*, London: Penguin, 1993, 4th edition.

Handy, Charles, *The Empty Raincoat: Making Sense of the Future*, London: Random House, 1995.

Held, David (ed.), *A Globalising World: Culture, Economics and Politics*, London: Open University/Routledge, 2004.

Hyett, Paul, *In Practice*, London: Emap Construct, 2000.

Jenson, Michael, *Mapping the Global Architect of Alterity: Practice, Representation and Education*, London: Routledge, 2014.

Kindleberger, Charles P. and Aliber, Robert Z., *Manias, Panics, and Crashes: A History of Financial Crises*, New Jersey: John Wiley & Sons, 2005, 5th edition.

Luder, Owen, *A Guide to Keeping out of Trouble* (RIBA Publications *Small Practices Series*), London: RIBA Publishing, 2001.

Maslow, Abraham H., *Motivation and Personality*, New York: Harper & Brothers, 1954.

Mavity, Roger and Bayley, Stephen, *Life's a Pitch*, London: Corgi, 2009.

Meades, Jonathan, *Museum without Walls*, London: Unbound, 2013.

Mirza, A. and Lacey, V., 'The architectural profession in Europe 2014', January 2015. Available online at www.ace-cae.eu/fileadmin/New_Upload/7._Publications/Sector_Study/2014/EN/2014_EN_FULL.pdf (accessed July 2015).

Moser, Cliff, *Architecture 3.0: The Disruptive Design Practice Handbook*, London: Routledge, 2014.

Newport, Cal, *Deep Work: Rules for Focused Success in a Distracted World*, London: Piatkus, 2016.

Pevsner, Nikolaus, *London. Volume 1: The City of London*, London: Yale University Press, 1997.

Rifkin, J., *The Third Industrial Revolution: How Lateral Power is Transforming Energy, the Economy, and the World*, London: Palgrave Macmillan, 2013.

Rogers, Everett, *Diffusion of Innovations*, New York: Free Press, 1962.

Rogers, Richard, *Eye: The Story Behind the London Eye*, London: Black Dog Publishing, 2007.

Sardar, Ziauddin, *Introducing Chaos: A Graphic Guide*, London: Icon Books, 2008.

Schon, Donald A., *The Reflective Practitioner: How Professionals Think in Action*, Aldershot: Ashgate, 1991.

Scott, L.L., *Architectural Practice*, London: Butterworths, 1985.

Sinha, Sumita, *Architecture for Rapid Change and Scarce Resources*, Abingdon: Routledge, 2012.

Soane, John, *Plans, Elevations and Sections of Buildings*, London: Gregg Publishing, 1971.

Sparke, Penny, *The Genius of Design*, London: Quadrille Publishing, 2009.

Syed, Matthew, *Black Box Thinking*, London: Hodder & Stoughton, 2015.

Toynbee, Arnold, *A Study of History*, New York: Oxford University Press, 1997.

Wigglesworth, Sarah and Till, Jeremy, *The Everyday and Architecture*, Profile 134, Santa Ana, CA: Academy Press, 1998.

Wilson, Colin, *Thinking About Architecture: An Introduction to Architectural Theory*, London: Laurence King, 2011.

Wright, David (ed.), *Thomas Hardy: Selected Poems*, London: Penguin, 1978.

Zumthor, Peter, *Thinking Architecture*, Baden: Birkhauser, 2006.

Further reading

Web references

These are all subscription-free sites, although some content may be for members only.

www.arb.org.uk
www.archdaily.com
www.archinet.com
www.architecture.com
https://autotelicarchitect.wordpress.com
www.bdcnetwork.com
http://blog.buildllc.com
www.designcouncil.org.uk
www.dezeen.com
www.liveprojects.org
www.ukconstructionweek.com

Journals and magazines

These are subscription-only journals; some are available online.

1 *Blueprint Magazine*
2 *Building Design*
3 *RIBA Journal*
4 *Architecture Review*
5 *Architects Journal*

Index

Page numbers in *italics* refers to a table/figure

accommodation vessel, Lerwick *127*
adaptation work 152
adoption rates 167
ageing populations 132–3
Ai Wei Wei 77
architects: continuing professional development (CPD) 27, 36; defined 25–6; as direct sellers of bespoke designs 26; employment rates 31; interests of and professional bodies 24–5; legal action against 36–7; protection of title of 21–3; public perceptions of 72–6; role of 9–11, 14, 45; self-expression and language of architecture 72, 75–7, 112–13, *114*; technical/delivery vs. concept architects 104, 163
Architects' Council of Europe (ACE) 32
Architects Registration Board (ARB): compulsory registration with 23–4; EU graduate registration 93–4; future role of 164; non-EU graduate registration 94; professional fees 36; regulation of architecture courses 23
Architects' Registration Council of the United Kingdom (ARCUK) 21–2, 23
Architectural Association 12, 101
architecture practices: business income 53; global practices 31–2; high-profile 31–2; interior design work 16; mid-range practices, future of 167; practice sizes 15–16, 24, 31; professional fees 36; winning bigger commissions 141; world's largest firms 31–2; *see also* business

architecture profession: adaptability of 45; Black, Asian and Minority Ethnic (BAME) in 37, 38; and business practices 12–14; creativity of 52; current standing of 4–5; emergence of 19–21; Farrell report 58; formalisation of 21; internal fragmentation of 16, 17; public perceptions of 67–9; publications on 2–3; relationship with art 9, 19, 75–6, 110–11; RIBA as body for advancement of 21; shift from public to private work 15, 16–17; as time intensive 26–7, 55; time keeping 53; women in 37–8
architecture schools: and basic business skills 112; course length and costs 91; cross-disciplinary collaboration 110–11; drop out rates 91; in EU super-universities 99; and everyday good architecture 110; graduate numbers 88; lack of practical focus, critiques 101–5; lack of research opportunities 100; learning by making 111–12; overseas students 98–9; participation and engagement practices 105; practice-led teaching 106; pupillage system 89, 90, 101; and real-world employment 114–15; RIBA Examination in Architecture for Office-Based Candidates 106–7; RIBA validation of 21, 23, 88–90, 104; role of small practices in student learning 93; seven year award (2016) 92–3; student population 87–8; studio (unit) system 101–3, 111, 119; sustainable development course content 104–5; 3 + 2 Bologna model 90; three part system of

178 Index

education 90–3; and time for creative exploration 109–10; *see also* education

art: application of 69; relationship with architecture 9, 19, 75–6, 110–11

Assemble 9, 12, 165

Aurelius, Marcus 119

automation 134, 162–3

autotelic, defined 1

autotelic architects 3, 162

autotelic learner 115–16

autotelic work 2, 49–50

Baggini, Julian 119

Baillieu, Amanda 71

Baker, Herbert 50

Baker, Laurie 56

BAME (Black, Asian and Minority Ethnic): in the architecture profession 37, 38; as students of architecture 87–8

Bank of England 49–50, *51*

Barbara Weiss Architects 59

Barfield, Julia 150, *151*, 155–8, *157*

Bašić, Nikola 132, *133*

Bauman Lyons architects 79–80

Beckham, Victoria 28

Béhar, Yves 165

Bingler, Steven 73

Birmingham railway station 68

branding 60, 71

Branson, Richard 162

British Institute of Interior Design (BIID) 16

Buchanan, Peter 81

Building Information Modelling (BIM) 27, 32

Bulfinch, Charles 21

business: architecture and requirements of 12–13; business costs and earnings 36; business management skills of architects 18; cash flow 54; charging structures 56–7; combined with creativity 50–2; economic efficiency and ethical practice 78–80; education in basic business skills 112; practice income 53

Byker Wall, Newcastle 17, 69

Capra, Fritjof 125, 126

Carbuncle Cup 70, 74

celebrity influences 28

Centre for Alternate Technology (CAT) 104

change: adaptability of architecture profession 45; key drivers for 38–9, 125–6; spirit of, Victorian era 45–6

charities 130–2

Chinese Embassy 78

Clark, Kenneth 9, 84

climate change: architecture's response to 126–8, 130–2; autotelic response to 130–2; carbon emissions from construction 128–9; flooding 125, 129–30; global effects of 41–3; Paris COP21 summit 40, 43, 104, 129, 146; and political response to 40; structural storm damage, London 42; threat from 125–6

collaboration: between architecture schools 99–100; autotelic working and 1, 128; with clients 161; cross-disciplinary collaboration 143, 165; cross-disciplinary collaboration, architecture schools 110–11; design collaboratives 160–1; and future working practices 158–60; and international work 32, 79; and societal change 165; and virtual platforms 161–2

collective decision-making 44–5

Collet, Jean-Luc *156*

Colombia 147

commercial work 2

community-based projects 107–9; see also Live pro

competition entries 18–19, 65

conservation work 150–2

construction: and ageing populations 134–5, *136*; carbon emissions and 128–9; forecasted growth 45; global market 147; green construction 155; healthcare facilities 141–3, *142*; output in the EU 32; poor conditions, overseas sites 79; schools 141; and sustainable development 39–40, 144; *see also* housing

construction kits 138, *140*

continuing professional development (CPD) 27, 36

contributive work 2

conversions 152

creative work 2

Crossrail projects, London 22

Csikszentmihalyi, Mihaly 46

Cullen, Gordon (mural) *11*

Index 179

Dali, Salvador 70–1
de Botton, Alain 2
design: bespoke design 26; design courses *102*; digitisation of design work 27; good design and value creation 60, *61*, 62–5, *64*, 69, 81; national economic value of creative industries 83; and public engagement 69–70, 75–6; public understanding/appreciation of 68–9, 71; social value of 83–4; undervaluing of 57–8, 69
Diller, Liz 114, 163–4
Dittmar, Hank 130
DIY architectural dialogue *114*
Doll, Clarence 14

education: acceptability of failure 116; commodification of 97–8, 117; and flexibility 119; and focus 119; income from overseas students 98–9; international collaboration 99–100; live projects 107–9; popularity of art and design 87; regulation of architecture courses by ARB 23; research funding 100; resilience and 117–19; risk-taking 116–17; studying abroad in the EU 97; super-universities, EU 99; tuition fees and loans 95–7; *see also* architecture schools
employment: employment rates 31; of EU graduates in the UK 93–4; graduate working conditions 94–5; of non-EU graduates in the UK 94
energy sources 155
environmental challenges 125–6; *see also* climate change; sustainable development
Erskine, Ralph 17
ethical practice: importance of 77–8; and overseas work 78–9; and sustainable development 79–80; United Nations Global Compact (UNGC) 80–1

failure 116–17
Fajardo, Sergio 148
Farrell, Terry 58, 110
fees: architect's fee and client value perspectives 58–9, 167; downward pressure on 13, 16, 53; free work vs. promotion 66–7; hourly rates 53; implications for future of architecture 167; pay and conditions 33–6,

37, 115; payment structures 53; value billing 56–7; *see also* salaries
fictional/unbuilt architecture 138
flexibility 119
focus 119
Foster + Partners 160–1, 165
Frank Lloyd Wright School of Architecture 111–12, *113*
FR-EE 160–1

global practice 32–2, 36, 147
Gombrich, E. H. 9, 168
Green, Harriet 54
Greenfield, Guy 143
Greig, David 69, 74–5

Hadid, Zaha 54, 135, 146
hand drawing 112
Hardy, Thomas 25, 28, 54
High Line Project, New York 152, *154*
housing: co-housing projects 165–7; and demolition of community buildings 28, *29*; elitism and inequality of new housing 77; on flood plains, UK 125; New Ideas for Housing competition 144–6; private housing 53; residential work 53, 56, 66; social housing, post-WWII 15, 16–17; student housing 141; in urban environments 144–6

iconic buildings 110, 147–8, 150
iMac computer *61*
India: architecture schools 88; Houses of Parliament, New Delhi 50; megacities 39
Institute of British Architects in London 21
interior design work 16
International Union of Architects (UIA) 89
Internet 40–1
iPhone 62

Japan 148–50
Jenson, Michael 33
jovoto 161–2

Khalili, Nader *139*
Krushchev, Nikita 4

180 Index

language: and architects' self-expression 72, 75–7, 112–13; DIY architectural dialogue *114*
Le Corbusier 54
legal profession 52–3
Lerner, Jaime 130
Lipton, Stuart 103–4
London Eye 150, *151*
London School of Architecture 96–7, 106
long hours culture 26–7, 53, 92, 115
luck 65–6

MacEwen award 81
Makiguchi, Tsunesaburo 2, 54, 60, 107, 115
Malone, Kate 160
marketing 59, 70, 164
Marks, David 150, *151*, 155–8, *157*
Martin, Sir Leslie 90
McEvoy, Mike 158
Meades, Jonathan 72
Middle East: architecture firms 24; climate change effects 40, 41; construction in 32, 146; satellite offices in 33
Mockbee, Samuel (Sambo) 9, 115
modernism 17, *34*
Morgan, Chas 14
Morocco 147
Morrell, Paul 25, 45

National Grid offices 62, 65
networking 52, 70, 83
Newport, Cal 54
Nichiren Daishonin 6
Nixon, Richard 4

Oasis office, London *108*, 109
O'Donnell, Sheila 163
Opéra Bastille (Bastille Opera House) 65–6
Ott, Carlos 65
overseas work: challenges of 79; cities of the future 146–7; dominance of largest practices 32–3; and ethical practice 79–80; in the Middle East 32, 33, 146; for smaller/newer practices 147

Paris COP21 summit 40, 43, 104, 129, 146
Patel, Amrish 116–17, *118*
Paxton, Joseph 65
Pevsner, Nikolaus 50

politicians: influence on architecture 27–8; lack of support for sustainable development 40
population changes: ageing populations 132–4; and inequality 125; resource availability and 39, 43; sustainable development design and 39–40, 144; urban design and ageing populations 134–5, *136*; urbanisation and population densities 144
pop-up architecture 135–8, *159*
post occupancy evaluation (POE) 59, 62–5
practice-based research 27
procurement 26, 141
Professional Experience and Development Record (PEDR) 93, 95, 107
professional indemnity (PI) insurance 13, 36, 66
public projects: framework procedures 26; procurement processes 26, 141; twentieth century 15, 16–17
public relations 69–72

Radic, Smiljan 141
Reading School of Architecture 111
refurbishment work 16, 152, 155
regulatory bodies 21–5
residential work: charging structures 56; free open source house blueprints 66; private housing and workload 53
resources: availability and population increase 39, 43; key drivers for change 38–9; and sustainable development 39–40; urban pollution and waste 39
retrofit work: and ageing populations 134; available work 16, 110; as sustainable development 40, 43, 152–8, *156*, *157*
Richardson, Henry Hobson 21
Rogers, Everett 167
Rogers Stirk Harbour + Partners 143
Royal Institute of British Architects (RIBA): advancement of architecture remit 21, 24; The Architect and his Office report 18; Architects for Change (equality forum) 38; and the architecture profession 5, 164, 167; benchmarking survey 15, 18, 37; Building Futures survey 24, 79; Client and Architect report 16,

53, 59, 163; Designing City resilience conference 132; Examination in Architecture for Office-Based Candidates 106–7; future role of 164; Future Trends survey 31; incubator spaces 36; Institute of British Architects in London 21; participation and engagement with design teaching 105; professional fees 36; RIBA building *20*, 21; seven year award (2016) 92–3; skills report (2014) 104–5; United Nations Global Compact (UNGC) 80–1; validation of architecture courses 21, 23, 88–90, 104

salaries: averages 36, 37, 53; salaries and costs of living 35; for staff 37; starting salaries 53, 94–5, 115; *see also* fees
schools of architecture 3, 14, 87, 88, 90, 91, 98, 99, 100, 103, 104, 110, 111, 112, 119, 167
Schumacher, Patrik 105
Sea Organ and Greeting to the Sun, Zadar, Croatia 132, *133*
self-concordant goals 1–2
Seligman, Martin 117–19
Serpentine Gallery 135–8, *137*, 141
the Shard 68
Shrinarayan Hindu temple in Neasden 116–17, *118*
Sild, Tiit 138
Skidmore, Owings & Merrill (SOM) 21, 33
small-scale architecture 135
Soane, Sir John: career progression 49–50, 163; and the next generation 87; professionalisation of architecture 21; on the responsibilities of the architect 14; Sir John Soane in a train toilet *10*; work records 71, 72
social inequality 125–6
speculative work 18
staff: mentoring and training 82; staff retention 37, 82–3; team creation 81–2; and time management 54
Stirling Prize 70, 74, 77, 141, 143, 144, 152
studio-L 160
Supermachine 148, *149*

sustainable development: within architecture courses 104–5; and the construction industry 39–40; design and population growth 39–40, 144; and ethical practice 79–80; and global systemic problems 125; green construction 155; impact of COP21 on 104, 146; lack of political support for 40; and retrofit work 40, 43, 152–8, *156*, *157*
Syed, Matthew 116

Tate Harmer *159*
technical architects 163
technology: automation 134, 162–3; and autonomy 164–5; collaboration on virtual platforms 161–2; and day-to-day practice 164; digital revolution 40; digitisation of design work 27, 164; and global practices 32; innovation and 38–9; transferable technology, sandbag construction *139*
Thailand 148, *149*
time management: long hours culture 26–7, 53, 92, 115; Pareto's Law 54; skill prioritisation and delegation 54; and types of work 54–6
Tochtermann, Wolf 103
Toynbee, Arnold 126
transient architecture 135–8
TREExOFFICE, London *159*
Tshumi, Bernard 119–20, 146
Tuomey, John 163
Turner Prize 9, 12

UAL campus for Central Saint Martins, London *153*
United Nations Global Compact (UNGC) 80–1
United States of America (USA): emergence of architecture as profession 21; skyscrapers, Chicago 13, 21
urbanisation: cities of the future 146–7; city-centre parks 144, *145*; megacities 39; and population densities 144; rejuvenation through architecture 148–50; and siting of new housing 144–6; spikes to deter homeless *44*; waste and pollution 39

182 Index

Valode & Pistre 147
value: and brand awareness 60; and desire for good design 60, *61*, 62–5, *64*, 69, 81; and luck 65–6; value billing 56–7; value creation 83; value systems as subjective 58
Venice *131*
Venice Biennale 75, 76, 141
Vesely, Dalibor 109–10

Wang Shu 107
Warne, John 23
Warne Report 23
waste, urban 39
Western-influenced spaces 33
Westfield Shopping Centre, London 28, *30*
Wigglesworth, Sarah 83
Wilson, Colin 9
Wilson, Paul 19, 138

women: in the profession 37–8; and qualification process 91
Women in Architecture 4, 38
work flow: future/current project balance 82–3; and procurement processes 26; speculative work 18; and staff retention 82–3
Wornum, George Grey (RIBA building) *20*
Wright, Frank Lloyd 111–12, *113*, 158, 168
Wundarland Kalkar, Germany 165, *166*

Young Architect of the Year Awards 168

ZAP Architecture 95
Zumthor, Peter 111, 135